Preface

Lawyers are society's primary architects of contractual relationships in a vast array of settings, yet standard law school casebooks provide little coverage of how contracts should be designed. *Contracting* presents an overview of the function of contracts and a tool box for designing effective agreements — contracts that will accomplish clients' objectives and avoid common pitfalls. The text includes numerous examples drawn from actual contracts, and a number of full-length contracts are included in the appendices. This Handbook is designed for use as a supplementary text for a first-year contracts course, and could also be used in connection with a legal methods course, negotiation course, or business planning course.

This Handbook is drawn from Foundation Press's textbook, *Analytical Methods for Lawyers*, which was created to accompany a course we and other professors have taught for the past five years at Harvard Law School. The course and the original text grew out of our joint realization that the traditional law school curriculum, with its focus on the development of analogical reasoning skills and legal writing and research, left many law students inadequately prepared for upper-level law courses and, more importantly, for legal practice in the modern world. Lawyers, whether corporate counsel or public interest advocates, must work in settings where effective argumentation and the giving of sound legal advice often depend on mastery of language and techniques derived from a range of disciplines that are staples of the modern business school curriculum, but notably absent, in introductory form, from law school classrooms.

True, a number of students arrive at law school well equipped with general knowledge of some of these areas from their undergraduate or work experiences. Equally true, however, is that many, perhaps the majority, of law students are woefully underprepared in these areas. They may self-select away from upper-level courses in which their inadequate preparation would severely disadvantage them. These students will graduate from law school without a set of basic skills, the absence of which will hamper their development in almost any of the careers that law graduates now pursue. Moreover, even those students who do have strong general preparation are often unacquainted with how what they have learned may be used effectively by practicing lawyers. It has been our experience that many students are themselves acutely aware of their deficiencies (or are made aware of it when they encounter certain discussions in first-year classrooms or when they receive their first assignments in a summer job or internship). Such students are eager to have their legal education enhanced by material like that in this Handbook, which promises to demystify analytical concepts and quantitative techniques that they see as clearly relevant to success in their law school coursework and, ultimately, to success in their chosen careers. It is primarily for these students that this Handbook has been written.

Unlike traditional introductory treatments, this Handbook is not a dry or technical text, far removed from the world of law. Quite the opposite. Virtually every concept is introduced, explained, and applied in legal contexts. Additionally, this Handbook is designed to be used to facilitate problem-based classroom discussion, materials for which are available to instructors in a Teachers' Manual. The translation from theory to practice is not left for students to develop on their own, after graduation. Instead, it is at the very heart of this Handbook.

Cambridge, Massachusetts
July 2004

Contents

Contracting

1. Introduction

Writing contracts is an important part of a lawyer's job. The bread-and-butter work of many lawyers is transactional. Notably, they make agreements for the production of goods and the provision of services, for the sale and development of real estate, for the licensing of intellectual property, for corporate deals, or for financial arrangements — all of which are quintessentially contractual. Such transactional work is common in the public sector as well as in the private sector. After all, government and non-profit entities spend more than one-third of this country's GNP, much of it to purchase goods and services, and they also manage massive transfer and grant programs. These expenditures are usually mediated by contracts. Additionally, lawyers involved in litigation of all types settle the vast majority of their cases. Settlement agreements are contracts in their own right, and they can be quite involved, whether in a business context or in a personal context (just think of divorce and custody agreements). Obviously, then, designing contracts is a major aspect of legal practice for most lawyers. Additionally, understanding contract design is valuable for lawyers engaged in litigation involving contractual disputes. So it's important for you to learn how to design the best contracts possible and how to analyze contract design.

Having an organized idea of the purposes that contracts serve, the problems that can arise after they're written, and the ways that these problems can be avoided is a good starting point for drafting effective contracts. For instance, a client who wants to have a building constructed might ask you whether to use a flat-fee or a cost-plus payment arrangement. Regardless of which is chosen, your client will want to anticipate the problems that could arise (e.g., under a flat-fee contract, the contractor might buy low-quality materials) so that you can incorporate into the contract provisions that will safeguard against these problems (e.g., specify in the contract what quality of materials are to be used in order to avoid the possibility that a flat-fee contractor will use inferior materials). In addition, your client will want to know what the legal consequences will be if the contract is breached (e.g., how damages will be calculated if the building isn't completed on time). Your client will also want to know whether including an arbitration clause would be wise. Thus, you'll also be putting to use your knowledge of contract law.

2. Why Contracts Are Made

At the most general level, there is only one reason why a person would want to make a contract: to obtain an advantage of some kind. Ordinarily, however, the other party would also want to make a contract in order to secure an advantage. Contracts, it would seem then, are typically made only because they are *mutually* advantageous.

Let's take a look at a few of the factors that make them so. The examples that we'll cover should help to illuminate the sources of the benefits that parties secure when they make contracts.

A. Differences in Valuation

In many contexts, the owner of something will place a lower value on it than another party will. For example, a homeowner who has to move to another city will place a lower value on his home than will many people seeking a residence in the area where he currently lives, and a business that installs new office furniture will no longer need its old furniture and will place a lower value on it than will another business that can use it. Obviously, when the owner of something places a lower value on it than another party does, it's possible for the two parties to enter a mutually beneficial contract for the transfer of ownership (or for lease). If the owner values the property she owns at $1,000 and someone else values it at $2,000, any contract under which the owner sells the property to the other person at a price between the two figures — say, $1,500 — will benefit both parties.

B. Advantages in Production

Often, one party wants an item produced or a service performed and finds that another party can do it more cheaply or more ably than he himself can. For example, a person may want his home renovated, and doing the work himself may be expensive in time and effort, whereas someone who makes his living from renovating homes can perform the work that the owner wants done at a much lower cost. Moreover, a specialist in renovation probably can do much higher quality work. Similarly, a restaurant owner may want a sign made, and a sign-making firm can do the job more cheaply and more elegantly than the restaurant owner herself can. In other cases, a party simply can't do what he wants done or can't do it very well. I may want my watch repaired but don't even know how to open it up. I may want my hair cut, but cutting it myself will be a disaster; my skill level just isn't anywhere near a professional's.

Why might a party have a cost or quality advantage that allows him to produce more cheaply or effectively than another? There are a number of general reasons: economies of scale in manufacturing an item, specialization in performing a task, having a particular ability or characteristic, to mention three of importance.

Clearly, when a task that one party wants done can be done more cheaply or better by a second party, entering into a contract for the task may well be mutually beneficial. For example, let's assume that I value a project that I can't do myself at $200 and that someone could do it for me for $100. Then I might pay this person $150 to do the job, and he'd be willing to do it for me for this amount. In such a case, all the elements for a mutually beneficial agreement are present, so it would serve both of us well to enter into a contract.

C. Complementarities

It frequently happens that two parties' capabilities mesh well in producing goods or performing services. For example, a computer software engineer who has developed a new product and a person skilled in marketing may, by joining forces, be able to offer the product, whereas neither alone could do so or do as well. Or a firm that specializes in drilling for oil and another that builds pipelines may combine their efforts and thus be able to bring oil to market more inexpensively and more profitably than could otherwise be done. When parties can increase joint profits by combining their complementary skills and capabilities, they're in a position to make a mutually beneficial contract.

D. Borrowing and Lending

An extremely common situation is for parties to need funds. A firm may want to initiate a new venture; an individual may want to purchase a home, send a child to college, or pay off a debt for medical care. At the same time, other individuals or financial institutions may be interested in lending or investing funds. In such settings, mutually beneficial contracts are possible. If one party obtains funds from another party on the condition that the first party repays the second party the amount borrowed plus interest or gives a share of the profits to the second party, both parties stand to benefit.

E. Allocation of Risk

Contracts may also be mutually beneficial when they allocate risk between parties, especially when the parties differ in their ability or willingness to bear risk. A classic case is an insurance policy, a contract between an insurance company and an individual or other entity. The insurance company is willing to insure the policyholder, who, in turn, is happy (or at least willing) to pay the premium in exchange for being covered against the risk. Investment partnership agreements are examples of another kind: the partners, as a group, are willing and able to take on the risk because it's distributed among them, whereas, as is often the case, no single partner is willing or able to absorb the entire investment risk.

F. Different Expectations

Predictions about the price of real estate, currencies, securities, and the like nearly always vary, at least to some degree, among parties. In such cases, parties may find it mutually beneficial to contract. For example, one party, expecting prices of real estate to drop, might sell to another party, one who believes that prices will rise. Or one party might buy futures in yen with the expectation that it will rise against the dollar, while another party sells these futures, thinking that the exchange rate will change in the oppose direction.

A point worth noting before we move ahead is that most contracts are not made for a single reason but for a combination of reasons. For instance, an agreement to produce may also involve elements of borrowing and lending, as is the case when the buyer advances money to the seller, implicitly giving the seller a loan, and in exchange obtains a lower price than if payment had not been made until the seller delivered on his end of the deal.

3. Principles and Checkpoints for Contracting

A number of fairly general principles and checkpoints are worth bearing in mind when you're making contracts for your client. The focus here will be on a few of the more important ones. They'll make many reappearances in the remainder of the chapter, as we put them to work in the context of specific types of contracts.

A. Enlarging the Contractual Pie

One of the most general principles of contract design is that the "contractual pie" should be as large as possible. The reason is obvious: the larger the pie, the larger the slice that can be given to each party to the contract and thus the better off each party will be. In other words, maximizing the size of the contractual pie is in the *mutual* interests of the parties; they both want it. This principle is important even when the other party isn't well represented:

your client will usually be able to benefit from any increase in the size of the pie that you can figure out how to bring about because you generally can come up with a way for your client to receive some of the gain.

In practice, the contractual pie is enlarged by including terms that increase the net value of the contract to the parties. Suppose, for example, that your client, the buyer of goods, has to have the goods earlier than the supplier would typically deliver them — say, December 1 as opposed to December 15. And suppose that the early delivery is worth an additional $3,000 to your client and would cost the seller $1,000 more. Early delivery thus creates an additional net value of $2,000 (i.e., $3,000 − $1,000 = $2,000) for the two parties and, according to the pie metaphor, should be mutually valuable to them.

But why, exactly, is it in the seller's interest to agree to delivery by December 1 if doing so will cost her $1,000 more? The answer is that your client, the buyer, should be willing to raise the price by enough to make delivery by December 1 worth the seller's while, because your client values early delivery more than it costs the seller. If your client offers to increase the contract price by, say, $2,000 for moving the delivery date up to December 1, the seller can be expected to agree to it. She makes an extra $1,000 in profit (the $2,000 increase in the price minus the $1,000 increase in cost), and your client is better off by $1,000 too (paying $2,000 for something worth $3,000).

The important lesson to draw from this example is that, whenever a term adds net value to a contract — when it adds more value for one party than it costs the other party — there will exist a way to include the term so that *both* parties end up better off. This is so because, as long as the additional value garnered by the party who benefits from inclusion of the term (e.g., the buyer in the example we just looked at) is more than the cost to the party hurt by its inclusion (the seller), it's possible for the first party to compensate the second party for more than the cost incurred and still come out ahead.

A kind of converse of this principle also holds: if a contractual term *reduces* the net value of a contract, it is possible to remove the term in a way that helps both parties. For instance, suppose that a delivery contract calls for special packing of the goods and that this method of packing costs the seller $5,000 but is worth only $1,000 to the buyer, who is your client. If your client offers to exclude the special-packing term in exchange for a price reduction of at least $1,000 — let's say $2,000 — and the seller agrees (which he would certainly be glad to do), both your client and the seller are better off than they would be otherwise: your client by $1,000 (price falls by $2,000 but value falls by only $1,000) and the seller by $3,000 (costs fall by $5,000 but price falls by only $2,000).

The take-home message is a very important one to bear in mind: a contractual term is in the mutual interests of the parties when and only when it adds more to the value of the contract than it costs. Indeed, most terms in contracts are included precisely because including them is in the combined interests of the parties: they add more to combined value than they cost.

The lesson here is that, when you're making a contract, if it lacks a term that you want or includes a term that you don't want, you may well be able to have the term included or excluded, respectively, by paying for it. By exploring the value of the term to your client and the cost of it to the other side, you can figure out whether your client will gain by paying the price it would take to induce the other side to acquiesce. Likewise, when the other party wants to include or exclude, you can determine whether the other party is offering enough to make it worthwhile for your client to agree. This principle is so central to contract design that overemphasizing it is virtually impossible. Indeed, much of what we'll be covering in the remainder of this Handbook can be viewed and understood as aspects of this principle: addressing contractual issues in a way that increases the total value of a contractual arrangement tends to be mutually advantageous to the parties involved.

B. Incentive Issues

When guiding your client through making a contract, you must be aware of the incentives that it creates. You have to ask yourself, Given the terms of the contract, what will the other side do if certain events take place? For instance, if you make a construction contract that calls for a fixed price, will the builder have an incentive to buy low-quality materials? If he's likely to, should you try to avoid that problem by specifying in the contract the quality of materials to be used? Or what if the contract contains a liquidated damage clause stating that $2,000 will be paid for a breach? Isn't it possible that this clause, intended to protect your client, could actually provide an incentive to the other side, the builder, to breach? For example, if completing the project would leave the builder with a loss of more than $2,000, wouldn't it be to his advantage to breach? If so, should you try to increase the amount of damages even though your client would then have to pay a higher price for the contract? Careful evaluation of the incentives — unintended as well as intended — established by the contract terms is vitally important when fashioning a contract. Doing so influences the value of the contract to your client as well as to the other party and may make other contractual provisions appropriate to include.

As important as it is to think about and evaluate the incentives in a contractual relationship, it would be an oversimplification to suppose that parties to contracts are driven solely by the desire for immediate personal gain. In fact, many contracting parties will want to behave in ways that are generally viewed as desirable, regardless of contractual incentives. They are prompted to behave correctly in a contractual context — that is, to adhere to contractual terms and otherwise act with good faith — by a belief that they have an ethical duty to do so or by a desire to protect their reputations (both in general and with regard to future dealings with current contracting partners). Nevertheless, most contracting parties are not saints. In many settings, assuming that narrow self-interest will significantly influence behavior is eminently reasonable. In such circumstances, it's generally better — often much better — for contractual terms to provide financial incentives that encourage productive rather than exploitative behavior. Even though we'll focus on immediate financial rewards when we address incentives a little later in the chapter, you should keep in mind that a sense of ethical duty or a concern for reputation often helps to ensure good results.

C. Uncertainty and Risk Bearing

Dealing effectively with uncertainty is another aspect of designing a good contract. In most contractual situations, there are numerous contingencies, and many will be problematic for one party or the other. So it's helpful to enumerate them and plan for them. For example, what if the contractor erecting the building for your client runs into unexpected costly problems? What if your client, because of a financial reversal of his company, wants to back out of the deal after the contract has been signed and the contractor has begun the work? You might want to include a provision that specifies how the building plans will be altered or, if the project is terminated prematurely, how much will be paid to whom. In other words, you have to think about how, in light of troublesome contingencies, to substantively alter the contract and allocate the risks.

D. Practical Enforceability of Contractual Conditions

For a contractual term to be workable — that is, for it to succeed in inducing the desired outcome — any condition on which it depends must be readily understood and its occurrence (or nonoccurrence) must be verifiable at reasonable cost. Let's suppose that a construction contract contains a term that excuses the builder from performance if the prices of material inputs exceed a specified amount. An adjudicator can readily verify whether these prices have indeed surpassed the threshold for nonperformance. Hence, the term is workable: if prices of inputs rise above the threshold level, the builder can abstain from performance and be confident that he would prevail in adjudication if the promisee sued for breach. Likewise, if costs haven't risen above the threshold, the other party knows that the builder can't use an alleged price increase to wriggle out of the contract.

But what if difficulty in digging the foundation is included in the contract as grounds for nonperformance? Such a term may be unworkable or impractical for the parties. On one hand, the foundation may, in fact, be hard to dig, but the builder may have a hard time establishing that it is, so the clause doesn't necessarily protect him. Demonstrating to an adjudicator that a foundation is hard to dig — perhaps because the builder encounters numerous stones that are difficult to remove or perhaps because water keeps leaking into the excavated area — may not be so straightforward or may even be impossible. On the other hand, if the foundation is, in fact, not hard to dig and the builder decides, for some reason, to claim that it is, the other party may be vulnerable because he may not be able to disprove the builder's claim. In either case, the parties may well face high litigation expenses in attempting to prove whether the requirements of the term have been satisfied.

Obviously, then, when you want to include a term in a contract that you're writing for a client, you must think about whether the conditions on which the term depends are readily interpretable and verifiable by courts or arbitrators. If they aren't, you may at least be able to figure out a way to make the conditions less difficult to apply — perhaps through an expenditure or an effort of some kind, for example, by specifying that an outside expert in construction be brought in to inspect the site and determine whether the foundation is hard to dig. This issue — of the kinds of conditions that can be interpreted and verified by adjudicators — is a very important one. Another point worth keeping in mind is that it is lawyers, not clients, who are likely to be knowledgeable about the feasibility and cost of determining the applicability of contractual provisions when disputes arise.

E. Disputes and Their Resolution

No matter how careful you are in crafting a contract, there's always a possibility that a dispute will arise. This is yet another consideration that you have to take into account when writing a contract.

One basic question for you to decide is whether to specify liquidated damages for breach of contract (i.e., to spell out what is to be paid to whom in the event of various types of breach) and, if you decide to do so, in what amount. As long as such terms are clearly delineated, they can provide definite incentives to avoid breach, and they can also minimize the costs of dispute resolution if a breach does occur.

Another basic question is whether to stipulate in the contract that disputes, should any arise, will be settled by arbitration rather than by the courts. Arbitration holds certain advantages for parties to a contract. It allows them to bypass the often expensive and time-consuming legal process of the courts, because the parties can determine the arbitrator and agree to the procedure (which often turns out to be a simplified one) in advance. It also allows the parties to have their disputes adjudicated by someone experienced in their field rather than by a judge or jury, who may know little about the subject of their contract. Because of these benefits, many contracts specify that disputes will be subject to arbitration. And the holdings of arbitrators are generally enforced by courts. Indeed, entire industries rely primarily on arbitration, and the practice is also widespread in international agreements.

Finally, you have to determine whether to include a choice-of-law provision — that is, a specification of which jurisdiction's law shall govern — in the contract. Many parties find it useful to do so, whether the agreement is to be enforced through arbitration or through the courts. Provisions of this kind may reduce uncertainty or enable the parties to avoid litigation over the issue in question. In addition, they may benefit a party involved in large numbers of contracts by providing economies of scale.

A later section in this chapter focuses specifically on these and other issues concerning disputes and their resolution, so we'll be coming back to the topic in a little while.

4. Production Contracts

Contracts for the production or construction of things are very common. They come in two classic types: *cost-plus* and *flat-fee*. Under a cost-plus contract, the party requesting the work pays the party doing the work whatever the costs turn out to be plus something extra. The "something extra" may be either a fixed amount or an amount based on costs (e.g., a percentage of costs). Under a flat-fee contract, the amount paid is fixed and is speci-fied in the contract. Suppose, for example, that your client signs a contract to have an apartment building that she owns renovated. If it is a cost-plus contract and specifies that the something extra is, let's say, 20% of the costs and if the contractor's costs total $150,000, your client ends up paying $180,000 (i.e., $150,000 + 20% × $150,000 = $180,000). On the other hand, if it's a flat-fee contract and it calls for your client to pay $175,000, this is the amount she pays, regardless of the contractor's costs or any other consideration.

Which kind of production contract would work better for your client? The answer is, It depends. Various features of the two types come into play, and you have to evaluate these features against the backdrop of your client's circumstances — to figure out not only which one is preferable but also whether certain kinds of provisions would be desirable additions. Several specific incen-tive issues as well as some of the other checkpoints that we covered also enter into the equation.

A. Incentives and Component Prices

A cost-plus contract contains no incentive for the contractor to find low prices for components. Let's assume, for instance, that renovation of your client's apartment building includes the pur-chase and installation of new windows. To find the best deal on windows, the contractor has the burden of searching for the best price, which may involve spending time on the phone or the Internet, driving to a distant supplier, and the like. So, if he's to be paid an extra 20%, let's say, on top of his total costs, what financial incentive is there under a cost-plus arrangement for him to go to all the trouble of finding windows at the lowest price? The answer is, None. Indeed, he may even have a perverse incentive to find high-priced windows: under this type of cost-plus contract, the higher the window price, the greater the contractor's profit. Suppose that the windows are available for $400 from a discounter but $500 elsewhere and the contractor decides to buy them at full price (i.e., $500). Your client winds up paying $600 for each window (i.e., $500 + 20% × $500 = $600) when she could have paid $480 (i.e., $400 + 20% × $400 = $480) apiece.

By contrast, under a flat-fee contract, the contractor has an incentive to search for low prices: because he receives a fixed amount regardless of the prices he pays for components, the lower his costs are, the greater his profit is. Let's say that the contract for renovation of your client's apartment building is a flat-fee contract specifying that the contractor is to be paid $200,000. He receives this amount — $200,000 — whether he pays $400 or $500 for the windows. It's to his advantage to get the windows for $400. Buying the more expensive ones would mean wasting his own money — in effect, paying $100 out of his own pocket for each one. So, without a doubt, he will install the $400 windows instead of the $500 ones.

As we can see, then, all other things being equal, your client may well be better off with a flat-fee contract. Under this kind of contract, which induces the contractor to search for the best prices, your client pays less to have her apartment building renovated than she would under a cost-plus contract, which rewards the contractor for paying unnecessarily high prices that ultimately inflate the cost of the project to your client.

Alternatively, you might attempt to circumvent the incentive problem caused by the cost-plus contract. One possibility is to include language in the contract that places a cap on how much the contractor can charge your client for various components of the project. For example, you might set a ceiling of $400 for windows in the apartment-building renovation. To do this intelligently, however, you have to know what is a good price for the component. For example, the price of windows is not likely to be something that you or your client knows with any kind of precision off the top of your heads, so you'd have to do some homework before specifying a $400 cap. Another possibility is to insist that the contractor get your client's okay on a price before he buys the component or that your client, rather than the contractor, be permitted to purchase it. But this approach also requires your client to know about current prices for the component and is often inconvenient. Hence, even though additions to a cost-plus contract may enable your client to lessen the problem — the lack of incentive for the contractor to search for low prices — they aren't likely to be sufficient to eliminate the problem or, even if they are, they may not be feasible to implement.

Up to this point, we've looked at things as if you're representing the person doing the hiring, and we found that a flat-fee contract tends to be better than a cost-plus contract for your client. But what does the situation look like from the other perspective? What if your client is the person being hired? Is a flat-fee contract likely to be better for this party as well? The answer is yes, and the reason is that the flat-fee contract lowers the total cost of the renovation project and, as we've already seen, enlarging the contractual pie ordinarily is *mutually* advantageous.

To see how a flat-fee contract can enlarge the contractual pie, let's focus again on a single aspect of the renovation project — the installation of new windows. The windows can be purchased for either $400 or $500. Suppose that both parties start out by considering two contracts for the project, one cost-plus and one flat-fee. According to the cost-plus contract, the contractor would pass on to the building owner the cost of the windows and would, in addition, charge a 20% fee. The flat-fee contract, on the other hand, might call for the owner to pay the contractor $550 per window.

Under the cost-plus contract, the contractor would, of course, buy the $500 windows in order to maximize his profit. Hence, the building owner would end up paying the contractor $600 for each window (i.e., $500 + 20% × $500 = $600), and the contractor would realize a profit of $100 on each (i.e., $600 − $500 = $100).

Now let's see what would happen under the flat-fee contract. The contractor would, in this situation, buy the $400 windows. He would make a profit of $150 (i.e., $550 − $400 = $150) on each one — $50 more than it would be under the cost-plus contract.[1] The building owner would come out better too, spending $550 per window (as specified in the contract) rather than $600. Given that both parties would do better under the flat-fee contract, they shouldn't have any trouble agreeing on which contract they should sign.

The take-home message, which we've encountered before, is this: if you can identify a contractual provision that is in the interest of the buyer and that increases the size of the contractual pie, this provision really will be in the mutual interest of the parties because it enables both parties to have a larger slice. This point is relevant to the rest of the material in this Handbook, but in the interest of expositional ease, we will not continue to repeat it. It is important, nevertheless, that you keep it in mind.

B. Incentives and Component Quality

As we just saw, under a flat-fee contract, the contractor has a financial incentive to find the best price for components of the job he's hired to do: doing so lowers his costs, thereby saving him money and maximizing his profit. For the same reason, this type

---

1. The cost of the contractor's effort in obtaining the windows at the lower price under the flat-fee contract has to be offset against the $50 gain per window. Let's suppose that this added cost is less than $50 per window.

of contract also provides a financial incentive for him to find the lowest-quality components (assuming that quality and price go hand in hand).

A cost-plus contract, on the other hand, contains no such incentive. The contractor passes the cost of components, whatever they are, on to the person who hires him, so he has nothing to gain by searching for low-quality components in order to keep his costs down. In fact, locating and purchasing low-quality products is to his disadvantage if the "plus" part of the contract is a percentage of costs. The incentive is, then, for him not to use components of low quality — or, in other words, for him to use high-quality and high-priced components. From the perspective of the hiring party, it's obviously undesirable for the contractor to have a motive to buy low-quality components, as is the case under a flat-fee contract. So a cost-plus contract seems preferable for the hiring party in this respect.

How can your client enter into a flat-fee contract and yet be protected against the problem of low-quality components? One approach is to insert a clause requiring the contractor to obtain your client's approval before purchasing components, such as the windows, for the apartments. This is a cumbersome process, however, adding time and trouble to the project. For instance, it takes time for the contractor to track your client down to get her okay. Or if the contractor happens upon a great bargain, he isn't able to make the purchase on the spot, and the opportunity may be lost because of the delay. In addition, the contractor — whose fee, as you recall, is fixed — may be concerned that your client will withhold approval unreasonably (e.g., by insisting on materials of extremely high quality) or try to extract some unrelated concession in exchange for approving a purchase.

Another approach is to specify in the flat-fee contract the quality of components to be used — for example, the brand and model of the windows. But to do this means that your client has to know, at the time you write the contract, what kind of windows she wants, which ones are of high quality and which ones aren't, and so forth. Gathering the information necessary to make such determinations in advance isn't always easy or practical. The investigation may well be time consuming and expensive.[2]

Despite these limitations, a contract term requiring advance approval of purchases or one specifying the quality of components can be helpful in many settings.

Even under cost-plus contracts, however, there is the potential for quality-related problems: quality may be *too* high. For instance, the contractor your client hires to renovate her apartment building may buy windows that are fancier and thus more expensive than need be. If he is to be reimbursed for his costs and paid an additional percentage, anything he does to increase his costs is to his advantage: increased cost translates into increased profit. Hence, he has an incentive to spend as much as possible on windows, even if their quality and price aren't justifiable from your client's perspective.[3] You can protect your client in the cost-plus contract just as you did in the flat-fee contract: by writing it in a way that requires the contractor to obtain your client's approval before buying the windows or that specifies the quality of windows he is to buy.

In summary, unacceptably poor quality is a risk under flat-fee contracts but not under cost-plus contracts, whereas unnecessarily high quality is a risk under cost-plus contracts but not under flat-fee contracts. Problems relating to quality of components that the hired person buys can be avoided in either type of contract by including language that requires purchases to be approved in advance or specifies the quality. Neither approach, however, is without its difficulties.

---

2. Note that, even though your client has to determine the appropriate quality of windows under an approval arrangement as well, the difference is that she doesn't have to do so in advance in this situation.

3. Another possible reason for the contractor to want to buy high-priced windows is to build up implicit credit with the appliance dealer — or to get a kickback.

C. Uncertainty and Renegotiation

Uncertainty is a fact of life, and it gives rise to several important issues that you have to consider when deciding which type of contract to go with, cost-plus or flat-fee. Contract renegotiation is one of them.

Suppose that your client's plans and desires change midway through the renovation project. She decides that a different kitchen configuration makes the apartments significantly more attractive to potential tenants or that recessed lighting is better than the standard kind. Under a cost-plus contract, your client's change of plans necessitates no (or very little) renegotiation, assuming that the contract permits your client to insist on some modifications. The contractor usually is willing to accept such a contract provision under a cost-plus contract. After all, he won't bear any of the extra costs himself. He would simply charge them to your client.[4] By contrast, under a flat-fee contract, you would have to renegotiate your client's contract, because you're asking the contractor to bear more costs than originally agreed on.

From the perspective of your client, the hiring party, renegotiation has two drawbacks. First, it's costly in time and effort. Second, the contractor most likely has an advantage over your client. By the time renegotiation becomes an issue, it's typically too late for your client to turn to someone else to complete the project (and the contract may well not allow this). Hence, the contractor already on the job is in a position to take your client for a ride in the renegotiation by charging her an unreasonably large amount. This is an example of what is often called a *holdup problem*. The need for renegotiation and the associated twin problems of costliness and holdup can be minimized by making sure at the

---

4. There's one qualification here: If the changes end up significantly expanding the renovation job and if the contractor's profit is a fixed amount (as opposed to a percentage, as in our example), the contractor, in addition to passing on the extra costs to your client, will want his own payment (his profit) to rise, so some renegotiation will be necessary.

outset that your client has thoroughly thought everything through and knows — and accurately communicates to you — what it is that she wants. But this process itself is costly. Furthermore, it's unlikely that your client (or you) can anticipate every change that she could possibly want to make down the road. All in all, then, in the face of uncertainty, the potential need to renegotiate argues in favor of a cost-plus contract over a flat-fee contract.

D. Uncertainty and Risk Bearing

Another issue associated with uncertainty that has to be taken into consideration is risk bearing. By definition, financial risk is borne by the buyer under a cost-plus contract. Whatever the costs turn out to be, low or high or anywhere in between, the buyer pays them. The greater the uncertainty, the greater the cost is for a risk-averse buyer. On the other hand, a cost-plus contract insulates the contractor from risk.

Under a flat-fee contract, the situation is reversed: the contractor bears the entire risk, absorbing the total costs, whether they turn out to be low or high, because his fee is fixed in advance. And if the contractor is risk averse and the costs turn out to be high, bearing them is a major disadvantage to him. But now the buyer is protected against risk.

Which type of contract is a better arrangement from the perspective of risk allocation (i.e., putting aside all the other issues that enter the equation)? The answer clearly depends on who is better able to absorb the risk. Suppose, for instance, that the risk is no big deal for the contractor — perhaps it's a large company that's involved in many unrelated projects, or perhaps it's part of a conglomerate enterprise. And suppose that the buyer is unable to bear much risk — maybe it's a fledgling business with meager assets. In this setting, it makes sense from the perspectives of both sides to use a flat-fee contract.

Conversely, suppose that the buyer is a large corporation and that the seller is a small construction company with limited assets and can't afford to take significant risks. Here, in terms of

Box 1
Flat-Fee versus Cost-Plus Contracts in a Nutshell

- *Flat-fee* contracts are often cheaper than cost-plus contracts because they induce contractors to search for the lowest prices (and their charges tend to reflect only these prices). The problem that prices will be too high under *cost-plus* contracts can be avoided by using price caps or requiring advance approval of purchases.

- *Cost-plus* contracts are often better than flat-fee contracts because they don't induce contractors to buy low-quality components to save money (though they may lead contractors to buy components that are too high in quality). The problem that quality will be inappropriate under *flat-fee* contracts can be avoided by specifying quality or requiring advance approval of purchases.

- *Cost-plus* contracts have the advantage of usually not having to be renegotiated when changes are made, whereas *flat-fee* contracts often do. Renegotiation is costly, and it subjects parties to holdup.

- *Flat-fee* contracts tend to be good on risk-sharing grounds when buyers are relatively risk averse. *Cost-plus* contracts tend to be good when contractors are relatively risk averse.

This list of comparisons of flat-fee and cost-plus contracts isn't exhaustive, but it does cover the most important points that you should take into consideration.

risk allocation, a cost-plus contract is desirable. The small construction company bears no risk and thus is more likely to agree to a cost-plus than to a flat-fee arrangement with the buyer. And the buyer willingly makes a cost-plus contract because it can tolerate the risk. (The buyer doesn't favor a flat-fee contract, on the other hand, because the construction company charges a lot to compensate for the risk it bears.)

E. Application: School Gymnasium

Suppose that you're the lawyer for a small private school that wants to build a new gym. The school is negotiating with a large construction company. What should the basic structure of the contract look like?

Before we get down to the specifics of figuring this out, two aspects of the general approach to drafting any production contract are worth emphasizing: (1) when you're deciding between a cost-plus contract and a fixed-fee contract, it's always important to think about the principles we've discussed, carefully considering them in light of your client's situation; and (2) whichever route you go, you should do everything possible to protect your client from the predictable kinds of pitfalls that we've discussed. Now let's work through the example methodically, taking into account our discussion points that seem most relevant.

A flat-fee contract seems good for the usual reason — it would motivate the contractor to search for low prices. Under a cost-plus contract, on the other hand, the contractor would lack an incentive to find low prices. This disadvantage presupposes that your client and its architect don't know enough about prices of the relevant components to be able to impose fitting price caps or require advance approval of purchases in order to ensure that the contractor secures good prices. In other words, the presumption is that your client doesn't know much about construction costs, the costs of materials, the best suppliers, and so forth. Thus, under a cost-plus contract, your fear would be that your client,

---

Box 2
Common Contractual Provisions

Can you relate the contractual terms in the excerpts below to points we've covered?

Flat-fee contract. The following terms are from a flat-fee contract between a city and a contractor:

> *Article 3.01. Contractor's Responsibility.* The Contractor shall do all the work . . . at his own cost. . . . [T]he work must be performed in accordance with the best modern practice, with materials as specified and workmanship of the highest quality, all as determined by and entirely to the satisfaction of the [City] Engineer. . . .The means and methods of production shall be . . . subject . . . to the approval of the Engineer. . . .
> *Article 3.03 Inspection.* The City shall have the right to reject materials and workmanship which are defective.*

Cost-plus contract. The following terms are from a cost-plus contract between a company and a contractor that calls for a fixed additional fee to be paid to the contractor:

> *Article 6. Authority of Company Engineer.* Company shall provide a competent Company Engineer, who shall have authority to direct all phases of work and to approve all authorized costs. . . . The Company Engineer shall have authority to reject work and material which [do] not conform to the contract. . . .
> *Article 8. Procurement of Materials.* . . . Contractor shall submit all purchase orders to Company for its prior approval. Company reserves the right to purchase any items directly on its own account. . . . Company also reserves the right to furnish materials and equipment from its own surplus.†

---

* Dib, 1994, chapter 3E-93.
† Dib, 1994, chapter 3E-71.

the school, will be taken to the cleaners. Your choice, then, would probably be to go with a flat-fee agreement.

If you do opt for a flat-fee contract, you'll have to protect your client against the possibility that the construction company will chisel your client on the quality of the gym it builds. For you to be able to ensure that the quality of the gym meets your client's expectations, your client would have to spend time investigating the ins and outs of gyms so that it can identify precisely what it wants and you can pin down the specifics in the contract. In other words, your client would have to spell out the details for the whole spectrum of components — type of gym floor, brand of fold-down bleacher seats, and type of shower facilities and heating plant, to name just a few. But because your client probably doesn't know very much about such things and their costs, the investigative task would be time consuming and difficult. On the other hand, it might be possible for the architect to provide plans that are sufficiently detailed to circumvent the quality problem. Under a flat-fee contract, you'd want to be as specific as possible so that the contractor wouldn't have an opportunity to shortchange your client on quality.

You'll want your client to think very carefully about its plans. Are they an accurate reflection of what your client wants? Can your client anticipate any changes that it might want to make down the line? Decisions are best made up front, because modifications made after work begins on the project would be add-ons to the contract that would require separate negotiation. So thinking ahead would really pay off in terms of saving time and trouble and expense later. Remember the holdup problem: if your client decides halfway through the job that it wants the gym to have a balcony with additional bleachers, the contractor, having your client over a barrel, might well attempt to charge excessively for the addition.

A flat-fee contact would mean that your client won't be bearing any risk. This may be a big advantage: your client can't really afford to absorb the risk because it might have difficulty raising additional money on short notice. Moreover, the construction

---

Box 3
What If Your Client Does Change Its Plans?

We've explained why a flat-fee contract is probably
best for the school and why, given this kind of contract,
it would be bad for the school to change its plans
during construction. Ideally, the school will think about
everything in advance. Realistically, though, it probably
won't. Maybe a new regulation will require a design
change, for instance. Think about this as a remedy:
any change in the plans will be paid for on a cost-plus
basis. What are the pros and cons of this supplement
to your flat-fee contract?

---

company, being large and easily able to absorb any risk inherent
in a project like gym construction, probably wouldn't charge a lot
more under a flat-fee contract to bear the risk of fluctuating construction costs.

In summary, it appears that your choice would be to go for a
flat-fee contract, but you'd make very sure that you specify in the
contract the quality standards to be met and, to prevent the need
to renegotiate the contract, that your client tries to anticipate everything that it's going to want.

By the way, how many of all these pros and cons do you think
the school will have considered? If you present your analysis and
recommendations laying out the kinds of issues just discussed,
it's quite likely that you'll contribute substantially to the making
of the right kind of contract, that you and your client can together
fashion a much better contract than otherwise.

F. Developing Arguments in Contract Litigation

What we've learned in this section is useful not only in drafting
production contracts but also in coming up with points to use in
litigation involving contract disputes. Suppose, for instance, that
you specified in the contract for the school gym that a certain

type of roofing material be used, a material recommended by the architect because of its durability. And let's say that the contractor chose an unusual, low-quality brand of roofing material that isn't particularly durable but which he claims is essentially equivalent to that specified in the contract.

A general term in the contract calls for "good faith" on the part of the contractor. You're thinking that this term might be interpreted in your favor to require the contractor to replace the low-quality material. At the same time, you're worried because the contractor might assert that your client made the flat-fee contract (rather than a cost-plus contract) so that costs (and the contract price) would be held down and thus so that he (the contractor) had a reason to economize — which he claims is just what he did. Given this possible counter to you, wouldn't it be better to make a more pointed argument than merely to invoke the duty of good faith and then throw yourself at the mercy of the court?

Armed with the principles we've covered, you could do so. You could answer the contractor with this argument: contractors have an excessive incentive under flat-fee contracts to choose cheap, low-quality components. Accordingly, your client attempted to avoid this problem by incorporating into the contract specific provisions to protect against being shortchanged on quality. This is, in fact, exactly why you specified the type of roofing material to be used. You can — and will — demonstrate that the particular brand of roofing material the contractor used is of very poor quality for your client's purposes.

More specifically, you might prove that the material could easily lead to a leaky roof in just a few years and that the necessary repairs would cost $30,000. You might also prove that the contractor saved only $5,000 by purchasing the low-quality material. Therefore, this unusual brand of roofing material isn't one that you would have agreed to had you discussed it, and the contractor, given his experience, presumably knew this. If the court rejects your argument, you can go on to say, then flat-fee contracts in the future will have a negative effect on quality that reduces the size of the contractual pie. Hence, a ruling against your client would cause contracting parties in the future to suffer: it will lower quality and reduce the willingness of buyers to pay for contracts, or it will require parties to spend excessive amounts of time and money drafting contracts that are incredibly detailed (e.g., by listing every brand that may not be used) in order to prevent behavior that isn't in their mutual interests.

This constitutes a more specific and more powerful line of argument to make to a court or arbitrator than does a general plea that your client was hurt by the use of low-quality roofing material and that it was simply bad faith for the contractor to have chosen the brand that he did. And it demonstrates how an understanding of the purposes of contracts and particular provisions within them can help you develop useful arguments and types of proof in litigation that might not otherwise have occurred to you.

5. Principal and Agent Contracts

A common situation is for one party, a *principal,* to contract with another, an *agent,* to do something: a person hires a lawyer to undertake a legal task; an individual hires a real estate agent to look for property; a store owner hires someone to manage the store; a taxpayer hires an accountant to handle tax matters; a landowner hires a farmer to grow crops; and so forth. A principal need not, however, be an individual. Indeed, when a company hires an employee, the company can be considered the principal and the employee an agent. Obviously, then, the principal-agent relationship covers a lot of territory.[5]

There are three major types of principal-agent contracts: *performance-based* (also referred to as *output-based*), *input-based,* and *fixed-fee.* Under a performance-based contract, payment depends

---

5. The production contract that we just considered can be regarded as a type of principal-agent contract, one in which the contractor is the agent. In our discussion, we addressed issues specific to the production context and focused on two particular types of contract, flat-fee and cost-plus. Here, we'll consider a broader range of issues, settings, and contract types.

on productivity as measured by some specified criterion. A real estate agent might be paid for making a deal, with the amount of the payment based on the sale price of the property. A store manager might be rewarded if the store makes a profit or if a survey shows an increase in customer satisfaction. A salesperson might be paid on commission, perhaps a percentage of the revenues on goods sold. A lawyer might be paid a contingent fee, a percentage of the recovery or settlement obtained, if any. These are just a few examples.

Under an input-based contract, on the other hand, payment is tied to input, such as time spent. For instance, a store employee or a lawyer might be paid on the basis of number of hours worked. Or a builder might be paid on the basis of his costs, as in the cost-plus construction contract that we considered earlier.

Under a fixed-fee contract, the agent is simply paid a stipulated amount for performing a service. Thus, an accountant might be paid a given sum for doing taxes, a lawyer for writing a will, a guide for providing a tour, or a builder for a construction project as in the flat-fee contract discussed earlier.

Many contracts are mixtures of these types, as in the case of a store manager who is paid a salary on the basis of the number of hours worked (an input) and also a bonus consisting of a percentage of profits (a measure of performance). For each general type of principal-agent contract, many decisions — such as what percentage of profits the store manager is to receive — have to be made to fully delineate the contract.

Performance-based, input-based, and fixed-fee contracts differ along a number of dimensions. In the examples that we discuss, we'll often assume that your client is the principal and decide from this perspective what kind of contract you should write.[6]

---

6. It's just for the sake of simplicity that we'll assume that your client is the principal. If your client were the agent, you'd end up going with the same kind of contract. The reason is one that should be quite familiar to you by now: the type of contract that's better for one party is also better for the other party — it's mutually beneficial — because it increases the size of the contractual pie.

A. Incentives

Principals generally want incentives to be created that will enable them to achieve their goals. The store owner or land owner will want to end up with a profit, the client will want her lawyer to win a large judgment, and so forth. It can't, however, be taken for granted that agents will do their best to advance the principals' goals. Doing so requires effort, which agents may not be inclined to exert unless they have an incentive to do so. Moreover, it's often insufficient for a contract merely to specify "best efforts," because such a term is hard to interpret and an agent's efforts may be difficult for a principal to observe and to demonstrate to a tribunal. Hence, understanding the incentives created by different types of contracts is important.

Incentives under a performance-based contract are, obviously, directed toward performance. Basing a store manager's salary on profits serves as an incentive for him to try to maximize the store's profits. Tying a lawyer's compensation to a judgment or settlement is an incentive for her to obtain as much as possible for her client.

The strength of incentives under performance-based contracts depends on the specific nature of the contract. Consider the store manager. If his compensation is but a small percentage of profits — say, 5% — he has little incentive to increase profits. In contemplating whether to work over the weekend on a new advertising plan that would bring in an extra $2,000 in profits, for example, he may well decide not to because he realizes that he'd end up with only an extra $100 (5% of the $2,000), too little to justify the additional work.

For the manager's incentive to be better aligned with what the store owner wants, he would have to receive a higher percentage of the profits. A 25% share — which would translate into an additional $500 in this instance — might be enough to induce him to work over the weekend. But even this fraction of profits isn't necessarily high enough: if he values an alternative for the weekend at $700 (e.g., he's already made plans for a vacation, and his airline tickets aren't refundable), he'd choose not to work for the store, because he'd end up losing more than he'd gain from the additional $2,000 in store profits. For the manager to have a sufficient incentive to maximize total value, he must be induced to spend the weekend working whenever his personal valuation of the weekend is less than $2,000. But this means that he'd have to obtain for himself 100% — the full $2,000 — of additional profits the store would bring in as a result of his weekend's work. Likewise, for him to have the proper incentive to prevent losses, he'd also have to suffer 100% of any losses the store experienced.

However, a contract in which the manager both earns any extra profits the store makes and suffers any losses it experiences might not be desirable for the principal and would often be unworkable. If the manager were to receive all the profits relative to some benchmark level, his earnings might exceed what the principal is willing to pay.[7] In addition, because the manager's assets might not be sufficient to cover the losses, it's possible that he couldn't bear them. Both of these problems might be unavoidable even if the manager's share of the profits or losses were less than — perhaps much less than — 100%. For example, if a manager of a large corporation were to receive 5% of profits, his salary could be hundreds of millions of dollars — an amount greatly exceeding what shareholders are willing to pay.

The upshot is that the strength of the incentive to perform under an output-based contract depends on, among other things, the percentage of profits or losses that the agent will receive or bear. Yet contracts under which agents receive high percentages of profits and suffer high percentages of losses may be undesirable for principals or unworkable.

---

7. To take this one step further, let's consider not just the manager, but all employees of the store. For each of them to have perfect incentives, each would have to be entitled to 100% of the additional profits — and the difficulty that this poses is impossible to miss.

An alternative way to create an incentive for the agent is to opt for an input-based contract rather than a performance-based one. A store owner might want the manager to work more hours than is customary because more hours means larger profits for the owner, so he would specify in the contract that the manager is to be paid by the hour. If the manager is specifically paid extra for working over the weekend, he'll be more willing to do so.

Typically, however, the number of hours that a manager works isn't the only determinant of store profits. How the manager oversees the workers, treats customers, and behaves in many other dimensions also enters into the picture. Indeed, envisioning a manager who spends much of his time gossiping with other employees, even though he does work long hours, isn't at all difficult. More broadly, a store manager rewarded only on the basis of time put in won't have an incentive to oversee employees effectively, provide good customer service, or attend to business rather than to personal matters. This exemplifies a general difficulty with input-based contracts: they tend to base payment on only some of the determinants of profits; hence, agents may not have much, or any, incentive to increase profits along other dimensions.

How can a principal attempt to ensure that the agent will perform as desired? The most direct solution is for the principal to pay to observe or otherwise assess the agent's performance. For instance, the owner of the store could hire a marketing firm to survey customers about their satisfaction. The information from the survey could be used to determine whether to pay a bonus or to decide whether to fire the manager. (Note that these uses of information introduce a performance-based element into the contract.) Such approaches to the problem of monitoring inputs that affect profits, however, are not only costly but also often provide only imperfect information about the inputs.

Finally, under a fixed-fee contract, there is no direct incentive for the agent to perform well. The principal may be relying entirely on the agent's good character, reputation, or desire for subsequent business from the principal. Or, as with the input-based contract, the principal could pay to monitor performance, perhaps making payment of the fee contingent on satisfactory effort or quality of the final product.

B. Risk Bearing

Another very important consideration in the choice of contract type is risk bearing — how great the risk is, who will bear it, and who is in the best position to bear it. Under a performance-based contract, the agent is the risk bearer (to the extent of the profit or other share), because random, unpredictable factors typically make it impossible for him to predict performance precisely. For any of a number of reasons, the store manager can't be sure what sales will be: consumers' tastes might change, competing stores might open, the weather might affect demand, general economic conditions might change, and so on. If he's paid solely a percentage of profits, his income could be very risky, fluctuating widely from month to month. Similarly, if a lawyer is paid solely a percentage of awards or settlements gained, her income might be very risky, because of the vagaries of settlement negotiations and judicial decision making. Hence, from the perspective of agents, performance-based contracts that create good incentives by tying compensation substantially to profit or output have a major drawback: they impose significant risks.

By contrast, input-based contracts tend not to impose risk on agents. A store manager paid by the hour knows, given the number of hours he works, what his salary will be. By definition, whether profits turn out to be high or low is irrelevant. A lawyer paid on the basis of the amount of time she spends on a case often knows reasonably well (though not perfectly, because some uncertainties are inherent in time spent) what she'll make. The size of the recovery the case produces for the client doesn't matter.

Fixed-fee contracts also may impose little or no risk on agents. However, when the required amount of effort is highly uncertain up front, the agent may bear substantial risk. Consider, for example, a lawyer who agrees to litigate a case for a fixed fee not knowing if or when it will settle.

Hence, agents who are risk averse tend to favor input-based or fixed-fee contracts, depending on the circumstances. Principals, though, bear risk under these kinds of contracts. The store owner bears uncertainty in profits if the manager is paid on the basis of time worked or a fixed salary. The client bears all of the risk in terms of the outcome of the case if the lawyer is paid on the basis of time worked or a flat fee. When principals aren't very risk

---

Box 4
Performance-Based, Input-Based,
and Fixed-Fee Contracts in a Nutshell

- *Performance-based* contracts create incentives for performance. But the creation of strong incentives requires that the agent receive a high percentage of profits and bear a high percentage of losses, which may be undesirable for the principal and unworkable.

- *Input-based* contracts also create incentives for performance. But to the extent that contracts of this type leave out hard-to-observe or hard-to-measure dimensions of input that affect performance, incentives for performance are incomplete. Such dimensions of input can sometimes be monitored, but monitoring is costly and often imperfect.

- *Fixed-fee* contracts don't create incentives for performance. Here, too, monitoring can sometimes be a solution.

- *Performance-based* contracts impose risk on agents, which is a drawback if agents are more risk averse than principals.

- *Input-based* and *fixed-fee* contracts tend to protect agents against risk, which is an advantage if agents are more risk averse than principals.

averse relative to agents, on the other hand, the parties tend to prefer input-based or fixed-fee contracts.

Although agents might generally be thought to be more risk averse than principals are, often the opposite is true. Suppose, for instance, that the principal is a plaintiff in a lawsuit who has little in assets and the agent is a successful lawyer or law firm with a large portfolio of cases. That an input-based contract protects the lawyer from risk and imposes it entirely on the client instead is a disadvantage rather than an advantage. A performance-based contract — for example, one under which the lawyer receives a fraction of the settlement or judgment — would be superior in terms of risk allocation. The client still bears considerable risk under a contingent-fee contract under which the lawyer receives, say, 33% of any recovery, but in the event of a loss, the client doesn't have to pay legal fees, which otherwise may have been large.

C. Application: Coffee Shop Manager

Suppose that you're the general counsel for a new coffeehouse company that aspires to be another Starbucks. You're working on a contract that will govern the managers of all the company's cafes. The following points are made during in-house discussions.

- The kind of person the company is looking for to fill these positions usually makes in the neighborhood of $50,000 a year in a salaried position.

- The job of manager entails hiring and firing, overseeing employees (e.g., monitoring their diligence and their behavior with customers), ordering supplies from the central warehouse and distribution system, among a host of other responsibilities (e.g., ensuring that the establishment is clean and opens on time).

- The company's computer system can track on a daily basis the receipts of each cafe and the costs

---

Box 5
Screenwriter's Contract

The following excerpts are from a principal and agent contract — specifically, a standard employment contract for a screenwriter on a British feature film. Can you relate the contractual terms to points we've covered? Try to identify why the various terms are in the mutual interests of the parties.

[The] writer undertakes under the Agreement to:
1. attend story conferences with the producer
2. carry out research and preparation for the script
3. write and deliver the treatment, first draft, second draft and principal photography script in accordance with the contract with the producer. Each manuscript should be clearly typed, and time is stipulated to be of the essence of the agreement
4. collaborate with others as necessary and render all reasonable services to the best of his ability. . . .

The producer will not be obliged to accept or pay for any work which is more than fourteen days in arrears of any delivery dates set out in the agreement with the producer [unless] it is by illness or incapacity of the writer.

Payment for the above is 23,200 pounds. In addition, the screenwriter will be paid [per use on] US network prime time TV, 13,000 pounds[;] ROW free TV, 6,000 pounds[;] UK TV, 2,000 pounds[;] . . . PBS, 1,500 pounds.*

---
* Mosawi, 1997, at 83–90.

of coffee and other supplies. In addition, you'll
know how many employees work at each location
and what their hourly wages are, and you'll be able
to track the number of hours they work each day.
The company expects to sell shares of stock to the
public in the near future.

What kind of contract should you write for coffeehouse managers?

1. Performance-based contract. The company's computer system, by tracking and calculating revenues and costs for the individual coffeehouses, makes it possible to determine profits fairly readily. So a performance-based contract that ties the managers' salaries to the profits of their respective cafes seems workable.

In considering profit-based compensation, however, you know that you have to be mindful of the risk that each manager will bear. True, someone who seeks a management position at a retail establishment is someone who's more than likely to take the initiative and whose risk tolerance is probably greater than the average person's. Nevertheless, a person like this may well not be interested in a position where salary is overly dependent on random elements that could affect profits. Applicants that your company really wants to hire might consider an entirely profit-dependent salary that yields $70,000 on average less desirable than the alternative of a flat $50,000 salary (which, as you remember, is the typical alternative for the kind of employee your company wants to hire). Even though the profit-based salary would be higher on average, the risk that income will at times be very low might be quite unattractive to these candidates. For example, the company's coffeehouses might really catch on, resulting in a salary of $120,000, or they might be a flop, yielding a salary of $20,000 (or even nothing).

In order to entice the applicants to serve as managers, you might need to guarantee a base salary — say, $40,000 — and augment it with a profit-based component, perhaps a modest percentage of cafe profits. (Observe that this approach combines fixed-fee and performance-based elements.)

If you decide on a profit-based component that you can reasonably expect to average $20,000, for example, a manager's salary would, in turn, average $60,000. Note that such an arrangement might be more attractive to applicants for the positions, because much less risk is associated with the salary, and that, at the same time, it would cost your company less on average: $60,000 instead of $70,000. The incentive for managers to maximize profits would, however, be weaker under this salary scheme, where the profit-based component is rather modest, than under the one where salary is entirely profit dependent.

Because your company is likely to go public, you also contemplate giving the coffeehouse managers stock options, which, it is commonly said, motivate managers. Perhaps each manager would receive options in 0.1% of the company's stock. But you wonder, given that you've been thinking about using profits as a performance-enhancing incentive, what additional motivation stock options would provide. You realize that stock options add essentially nothing to this incentive. The reason is that, because the company will be opening many coffee shops, the value of the stock of the whole company won't be affected in any significant way by the actions of a single store manager. Moreover, each manager would be given options to but a trivial percentage of the company's stock. Nevertheless, the stock options are a very risky form of compensation. Hence, on reflection, the case for including stock options in the managers' compensation packages seems weak.

2. Input-based contract. You're well aware that managers can affect profits of their cafes in many ways through their actions, behavior, and work style — that is, their input. The number of hours that managers work, for example, definitely bears on profits, so the contract should address this issue. It should probably include as well terms dealing with things that you want the managers to have an incentive to do. Unfortunately, a lot of this won't be observable or verifiable to a tribunal. For instance, profits will be affected by how well the staffs serve customers — how professionally, efficiently, and courteously they do their jobs. And it will be the managers' duty to ensure that their staffs perform appropriately — by making sure not only that their staffs understand what's expected of them but also, through direct supervision, that they are in fact doing their jobs at the level expected. In other words, the managers will have to be skilled at handling and motivating employees. Obviously, it isn't easy to monitor and evaluate such aspects of managerial effort. One way to evaluate managerial behavior — a costly one — would be through unannounced spot checks by company representatives posing as customers. But then you'd have to take this cost into account.

3. Fixed-fee contract. You could, of course, just offer managers a fixed salary of $50,000. They would bear no risk, but neither would they have an incentive to exert effort. The company could employ monitoring of inputs and performance to improve manager behavior under this kind of contract.

4. Your decision. After considering all of these points, you'll probably want to write a contract that has some performance-based component, probably in the form of percentage of coffee-shop profits. And you may also want to build into the contract one or more input-based components — at the least, one tied to amount of time spent working at the cafe. Note that under this contract managers must be compensated for the risk that they would bear owing to the performance-based component. Yet the higher cost would be worthwhile for the fledgling company if, as seems likely, the quality of managers' efforts will be important to the success of the coffeehouses. (See Box 6.)

6. Other Types of Contracts

There are, of course, many important types of contracts in addition to the two we've discussed, and we'll take a brief look at sev-

---

Box 6
Coffeehouse Manager's Contract

Managers of coffee shops of a well-known chain receive a base salary and are eligible for two types of bonus. A profit bonus is paid if the profits of a shop exceed a target figure, which is set on the basis of the shop's past performance. This kind of bonus is paid quarterly and is capped at 20% of the manager's base salary. A "snapshot" bonus is based on an evaluation, as reflected in the report of a secret shopper, of the store's adherence to the company's official policies. It can potentially be almost as large as the maximum profit bonus. All bonuses are split — 70% and 30% — between the manager and the assistant manager, both of whom also receive sizable discounts on merchandise, including coffee.*

---

* David Cope, interview with a manager, January 2000.

---

eral of them. The goal isn't to be comprehensive. Rather, it's to illustrate that, for each type of contract, you have to think about the general factors in the checklist set out earlier in the chapter and how to apply them. (Recalling the reasons we discussed earlier about why contracts are made, try to explain why those we are about to discuss were agreed to.)

A. Joint Undertakings

A partnership agreement among a group of lawyers or physicians; an agreement between two drug companies under which one is to develop a new drug and the other is to market it; a contract among a group of investors to start a company, where one takes on a primary managerial role; an agreement between a venture capitalist with many connections and with know-how in the business world and an inventor with relatively little business experience — these are just a few examples of contracts made by parties that want to engage in *joint undertakings* — in which possibly many parties do different things. Such agreements are as common as they are varied. And they are much more general than either production or principal-agent contracts, both of which involve "joint" undertakings in which only one party is doing something.

Incentives are important in contracts that govern joint undertakings. What you must think about in particular is what each party has to be motivated to do. For a partnership among lawyers where all the partners are in roughly the same situation, for example, you'd have to build into the agreement incentives for each to bring in new clients and to work hard and succeed. One way to do this would be by linking compensation to the generation of new business and to the number of hours worked. In the agreement between the two drug companies, on the other hand, you'd want the incentives you fashion to be very different for the two companies, because they have distinct roles (one is to develop the drug, and the other is to market it). Hence, you must think about what specific provisions you can include in the contract that will furnish effective incentives for each company. Perhaps the company that is to develop the drug should receive a payment based on whether and when the drug is approved by the FDA, and perhaps the payment to the marketing company should be based on drug sales revenue net of advertising costs.

Other considerations when you're drafting joint-venture contracts are uncertainty and risk sharing, which vary widely from context to context. For instance, in a partnership agreement among lawyers, the risk of a low salary may be a concern. To get around this problem, you might be tempted to draw up a contract in which the partners share profits more evenly than they would if rewards went to those who brought in business or worked long hours during the year. This approach would shield individual partners from excessive risk, but it would also compromise incentives. So including some input-based or performance-based features in the contract would be necessary.

Risk may have to be allocated in the drug companies' joint venture as well. If the drug-developing company is a relatively small firm with low assets, it wouldn't be well suited to absorb the substantial risks attending the development, testing, and approval processes. The contract you design would have to call for the large marketing company to bear a substantial fraction of these risks. Because this approach would dilute the incentives of the small company, you might have to set up contractual mechanisms that would allow the large company to monitor the small company's effort level.

These examples also serve to illustrate another point that we've covered: whether or not a behavior is observable and can be verified to a tribunal is important. Can the small company's efforts to develop a drug of high quality, to develop it quickly, and so forth really be determined by outsiders? If experts in drug development were hired to monitor the small company's progress, would this monitoring be sufficient? And how much would it cost? Can the expenses incurred by the small company in developing the drug be ascertained with any degree of accuracy? (If it buys a centrifuge and claims that it's for use in the development of the drug in question, how can the large firm know whether this is true?) Issues concerning the ability to observe or measure variables that you'd like to include in a contract are important, and you have to think about them in detail in advance in order to figure out whether they are, in fact, workable and appropriate to incorporate as terms in the contract you're preparing.

B. Sale or Lease of Property

Another prevalent kind of contract is one in which property is conveyed, either in a sales transaction or in a lease. For these contracts, too, incentives of various sorts enter into the equation.

Parties that are planning to buy or lease property are often con-

---

Box 7
Law Firm Partnership Agreements

The following excerpts are from samples of two types of law firm partnership arrangements. Think about them and, in particular, compare them in terms of incentives and risk allocation.

Formula schedule for distribution of earnings. One arrangement begins by defining a number of terms, including the following:

> *"Work credit"* shall mean . . . eighty-five per cent (85%) of the gross fees allocated to a . . . Partner or associate for legal services. . . . *"Associate profit"* shall mean the excess of associates' work credit over all associates' direct expenses. . . . *"Client credit"* shall mean the amount added to the participation of a . . . Partner . . . based on clients attributable to such Partner. . . . *"Participation"* shall mean the total share of each Partner in the profits of the Firm.

The contract then goes on to specify what the partners will earn:

> Each Partner is guaranteed a minimum participation . . . of $ ___ in each fiscal year. . . . The normal participation of each Partner shall be the sum of the following: . . . work credit; . . . client credit . . . ; per capita share of other firm profits; per capita share of associate profit.*

Equal partners system. Under an equal partners arrangement, the partners, it stated in the sample contract, "shall have equal allocations of firm profits . . . during each year." According to the commentary that accompanies the sample,

> [T]he equal partners system is probably used most often by newer or smaller law firms. It implies that the participants are in practice for better or worse with the intention to share the burdens and the rewards equally. The goal of such a system . . . is to make the partner with higher objective statistics aware of the importance the law firm places on the different set of contributions of a partner with lower statistics. Conversely, such a compensation system encourages the partner with lower statistics to close the gap . . . [with] the partner who has contributed more statistically.†

What do you think of this reasoning?

---

* Corwin and Ciampi, 1998, Section 5.04[2].
† Corwin and Ciampi, 1998, Section 5.04[3].

cerned about its condition. This is an issue that you can address directly by contractual terms. For example, if your client wants an apartment to be clean, the hot water to be hot, and so forth, you can specify as conditions in the contract that these criteria are to be met. If your client is purchasing a home, you might condition the deal on an inspection of the property as of a particular date. Including a term like this gives the other side a clear incentive to make sure that the home remains in good condition for your client.

On the other side of the coin, a lessor might like to have some assurance that the lessee will maintain the property in good condition during the period of a lease. If you represent the lessor, you can include contractual terms that deal directly with this matter and supplement them with provisions that, for example, give your client the right to inspect the property while the lease is in effect, require the lessee to put down a security deposit to cover the cost of repairs should they be necessary, and impose a penalty on the tenant (such as termination of the lease) for failure to maintain the property. Should your client (the owner) not want to allow the property to be sublet (e.g., because of the possibility that the sublessor would be less careful than the lessor), you can specify this in the contract too.[8]

For contracts covering the delivery of goods, you might want to think about incentives aimed at reducing the chance that the property will be damaged during transport. All other things being equal, it would be appropriate for the risk of harm or loss to be borne by the selling party, as that party packs the goods and arranges for them to be transported. A contract term specifying this would motivate the seller to take proper precautions.

The incentive issue is very different when it comes to the matter of disclosure. Often, one side — usually the seller but sometimes

---

8. In practice, when determining whether to grant a lease, property owners typically assess prospective lessees on a number of dimensions to judge how likely they are to maintain the property or to disturb other tenants.

the buyer — has information that the other side doesn't have about the condition of the property. For example, the seller but not the buyer might know that toxic wastes have been dumped onto a parcel of land or that the basement of a house leaks. In such a case, the knowledgeable party would have an incentive to withhold unfavorable information — and might not be required by law to disclose it. It's always important to keep this possibility in mind.

Box 8
Apartment Rental Agreement

Why would the following terms be in a rental agreement for an apartment?

The Lessee shall not paint, decorate or otherwise embellish and/or change . . . the leased premises. . . . No washing machine, air-conditioning unit, space heater, television aerials . . . shall be installed without the prior written consent of the Lessor. . . .

The Lessee shall maintain the leased premises in a clean condition. . . .

The Lessor may enter upon the leased premises to make repairs thereto, to inspect the premises, or to show the premises to prospective tenants. . . .

The Lessee shall not assign nor underlet . . . the leased premises . . . without first obtaining the assent in writing of the Lessor.

You could protect your client (the buyer) with contracting options that provide for disclosure, require inspection, spell out guarantees that allow your client to seek redress if particular adverse circumstances arise, and so forth. For example, you might include a term specifying that the seller of land will indemnify the buyer for any environmental cleanup costs that turn out to be necessary.

Many kinds of risk are associated with the transfer of property. Being thorough in identifying and assessing them will help you figure out how they would best be allocated. If you're the buyer's lawyer, risks related to titles, liabilities (e.g., for environmental harms), and loss or theft of property prior to delivery are particularly relevant. Another risk is that the seller will turn around and sell to someone else, breaching the contract. If you represent the seller, on the other hand, you'd want to anticipate that the buyer might try to back out of the deal — because of a simple change of mind, a financial reversal, or a chance to take advantage of a better opportunity. In addition to specifying in the contract who is to bear what risks, you might also want to suggest that your client insure against some of them — say, by arranging for title insurance or liability coverage. Assigning risk will, of course, also affect incentives. (As we saw just a minute ago, for example, the selling party that packs the goods can be expected to do a better job if it bears the risk of harm during transport than if it doesn't.) The parties may, however, have different capacities to bear risk or abilities to insure against it.

C. Loan Contracts

Loans, which constitute yet another category of contract, are an omnipresent feature of economic activity: individuals borrow and lend and so do businesses, nonprofit institutions (e.g., museums, schools), and governments. The kinds of incentive issues that borrowers and lenders face are numerous, and we'll look at just a few, first from the perspective that your client is the lender and then from the perspective that your client is the borrower.[9]

One thing you'd want to take into account in looking out for a lender's best interests is that the borrower might sell his assets

---

9. Other financial arrangements, such as taking an equity stake in a firm, raise similar concerns, but in the interest of brevity, we'll restrict our focus to loans.

and end up being unable to pay off the loan. To guard against this possibility, you could take out security interests (such as a mortgage) or employ covenants (i.e., clauses that would, for example, prohibit the sale of assets without your client's permission). Another approach would be to put controls on the borrower's expenditures (e.g., by including in the contract a covenant requiring the borrower to obtain your client's permission before making significant outlays).

You'd also want to anticipate the possibility that the borrower will seek out particularly risky opportunities, thinking that everything will be rosy if he succeeds but knowing that bankruptcy is a fallback if he fails. Should the deal not pan out for the borrower, however, your client will be left without repayment. You could address this problem of excessive risk taking through contractual terms that allow your client to control the borrower's investment decisions.

However, the degree to which the borrower's activities can be controlled by your client is limited. Moreover, your client wouldn't want to impose such constraints that the borrower would be prevented from conducting business reasonably well (thereby jeopardizing repayment of the loan) — or, indeed, be dissuaded from taking out the loan in the first place.

No matter how many precautions you take to ensure that the borrower will be able to repay your client, bankruptcy remains as a possibility, and you might want to provide for this eventuality in the contract. To the extent that commercial and bankruptcy law doesn't already adequately protect your client and allows you to contract for additional protection, you could incorporate terms that prevent other creditors from seeking and receiving priority over your client for repayment.

If you were representing the borrower, on the other hand, many of your concerns would mirror those of the lender's lawyer (e.g., ones having to do with controls over the borrower's monetary outlays and business decisions). You should keep in mind that restrictions on your client are not an unmitigated evil, however.

In fact, without them, your client might not be able to borrow at all, or the lender might insist on a higher interest rate to compensate for the greater risk of default. If this strikes you as being another illustration of our recurring theme — that enlarging the contractual pie is mutually beneficial to the parties, even if the term that enlarges it (viewed in isolation) is disadvantageous for one party — you're right on the mark. The party for whom the term is unfavorable can be compensated by the other party in exchange for agreeing to include the term in the contract. In the

---

Box 9
Loan Contract Secured by a Home

Why would the following provisions appear in a standard loan contract secured by a home?

Borrower shall keep . . . the Property insured against loss by fire . . . and any other hazards, including floods, . . . for which the Lender requires insurance. . . . The insurance carrier shall be chosen by the Borrower subject to the Lender's approval. . . .

Borrower shall occupy . . . and use the Property as Borrower's principal residence within sixty days . . . and shall continue to occupy the Property . . . for at least one year. . . . Borrower shall not destroy, damage or impair the Property. . . .

If Borrower fails to perform covenants . . . then Lender may do . . . whatever is necessary to protect the value of the Property and Lender's rights. . . .

Lender . . . may make reasonable entries upon and inspections of the Property. . . .

. . . Any forbearance by Lender in exercising any right or remedy shall not be a waiver or preclude the exercise of any right or remedy.*

---

* Lefcoe, 1997, at 1407–1420.

case at hand, in exchange for yielding some control over its own operations, the borrower (your client) is compensated by the lender with a lower interest rate than would otherwise be prudent. In this context, the interest rate functions as the price.

From your perspective as the borrower's lawyer, other issues might warrant consideration as well — for example, early repayment of the loan. Having the option to repay without penalty might be worthwhile in some circumstances: perhaps your client will have the opportunity to refinance through a cheaper source or will earn a great deal more than anticipated. Early repayment can be undesirable for the lender, however, so including such a term would make sense only if the advantage to the borrower outweighs the disadvantage to the lender.

7. Resolving Contractual Disputes

As a lawyer drafting a contract, you naturally have to anticipate problematic outcomes and legal trouble down the road and figure out how to avoid such pitfalls or, should they arise, how to handle them. Contingent provisions, damages for breach, and arbitration are three tools that you have at your disposal to help you do just this.

A. Contingent Provisions

Some potential problems that might lead to disputes can be avoided through the use of contingent contractual provisions. If you carefully think about a problem that could arise, you'll often find that you can write a contingent provision that addresses the issue and thereby heads off a dispute. Suppose that your client is a small firm that makes components for a GM plant and that GM is entering into a contract with your client for a steady supply of electronic parts. If workers at your client's factory go on strike, however, your client may need its obligation to supply these parts to be suspended because having to raise the cash to pay damages would disrupt its business. By thinking ahead, you can include in the contract a clause that excuses your client in the event of a

---

Box 10
Apartment Rental Agreement
and Construction Contract: Contingent Terms

Why is the following term from an apartment lease in the mutual interests of the parties?

Fire, Other Casualty. If the leased premises . . . shall be destroyed or damaged by fire . . . then this lease . . . shall terminate at the option of the Lessor. . . . If this lease . . . is not so terminated . . . then in case of any such destruction . . . rendering [the apartment] . . . unfit for occupation, a just proportion of the rent . . . shall be suspended or abated. . . . If the leased premises have not been restored by the Lessor . . . within thirty days . . . the Lessee may terminate this lease.*

How well do you think the following two contingent terms from a standard cost-plus construction contract would function?

29. Delay. Contractor will be excused for delay caused by inclement weather, labor disputes, acts of public agencies . . . or other events beyond the reasonable expectation and control of Contractor. . . .

30. Unanticipated Concealed Conditions. In the event that Contractor encounters adverse concealed conditions that could not reasonably have been anticipated, the Guaranteed Maximum Cost will be equitably adjusted, and the cost of dealing with such unanticipated conditions will become a Cost of the Work.[†]

---

* Lefcoe, 1997, at 1407–1420.
† Acret, 1990, at 47.

strike. The cost to your client shouldn't be very high if a strike is unlikely, yet the clause may be a very important protection for your client if a strike does take place.

The more contingencies you plan for in advance, the better off your client will be. Contingent provisions are not without costs, however. So you'll want to be somewhat selective and address a contingency only if its likelihood and its importance are sufficient to justify the additional effort in negotiation and drafting. In addition, for each contingency you're concerned about, you'll want to use your general knowledge of contract law to estimate how likely a tribunal would be to interpret a simpler contract (one without the contingency provision) in a way that would suit your client's needs just as well (e.g., maybe a tribunal would excuse your client should a strike occur even if the contract didn't mention this contingency). Of course, relying on a tribunal's fixing your contract can be risky and result in greater litigation costs.

B. Damages for Breach

The issue of damages for breach of contract becomes important when certain types of contingencies arise. If breach occurs and you haven't specified in the contract that damages are to be paid and how much they'll be if breach should occur, the tribunal will decide the amount. In such cases, damages are usually expectation damages as calculated by the court (typically by a jury) or by an arbitrator. But, as we've already briefly discussed, it's often in your client's interest to specify the level of damages — that is, to name liquidated damages — in the contract rather than to risk having others determine the amount of damages in the event of breach. (Keep in mind, however, that if liquidated damages are set too high in relation to what expectation damages would likely be, they might not be enforceable, because the court will regard them as penalties. So you are, in practice, constrained in the level of liquidated damages that you can set.)

An important advantage of specifying liquidated damages for breach is that doing so can result in savings for the parties at the time of a breach. When the parties name the level of damages in advance, the amount to be paid in the event of breach is clear. When they don't, the level of damages is often contested, and more resources than necessary end up being consumed to resolve the disagreement, and more uncertainty is introduced into contractual disputes.

In setting the level of liquidated damages, you have to think about several factors. One is the effect that the level you decide on will have on performance. The prospect of having to pay damages spurs performance. So breach is less likely if damages have to be paid than if they don't. Having to pay damages when delivery is late, for instance, serves as an incentive for the supplier not to miss the delivery date and thereby lessens the odds that delivery will be late. More specifically, the effectiveness of damages in preventing breach goes hand in hand with the level at which they're set: at a low level, damages aren't very effective and not very likely to prevent breach; at a moderate level, they're somewhat more effective and somewhat more likely to prevent breach; and at a high level, they're very effective and very likely to prevent breach, often even when performance would be very expensive or disadvantageous to the promisor. Hence, the goal is to set damages at a level that's mutually advantageous: high enough to ensure performance as long as performance makes sense but not so high as to elicit performance once performance no longer makes sense. The challenge is for you to figure out what this level is.

Thus, incorporating liquidated damages into the contract allows you to fine-tune the incentives for performance so that they match your client's needs. If late delivery would be very costly to your client, setting damages high for breach might be desirable in order to maximize the likelihood of timely delivery.

Another function of damages, including liquidated damages, is to protect the party that is the potential victim of breach from risk. Whether such protection is mutually desirable depends on whether and the extent to which the potential victim is risk averse.

For instance, a large firm might not be in obvious need of this kind of protection, whereas the insurance aspect of damages might be very valuable to a small, risk-averse firm that's really counting on performance (perhaps because it's barely eking by and faces ruin if the other party commits breach). For a very risk-averse party that might have to commit breach, on the other hand, the very possibility of having to pay damages constitutes a risk. Hence, not having to pay any damages when performance would be onerous — that is, being excused from having to meet contractual obligations under certain circumstances — might be desirable on grounds of risk bearing. In any event, we can see that naming liquidated damages in a contract allows you to select the degree of protection against risk that meets your client's needs.

The level at which damages are set also affects the contract price. The greater the damages that a promisor would have to pay for committing breach, the higher the price that the promisor will insist on at the outset. The higher price is, in effect, compensation for the higher risk that the higher level of damages reflects. If your client wants the contractor to pay very high damages for committing breach, the contractor may well want your client to pay a much higher price. As discussed previously, you should be setting liquidated damages at a level that's mutually advantageous; if you do, then there should be a contract price adjustment that leaves both you and the other party better off.

When you're drafting contracts for your clients, it's important that you think about all of these aspects of damages in general and liquidated damages in particular.

C. Arbitration

Another significant issue when a legal dispute arises is whether it will be resolved through arbitration or by the courts. It should be noted at the outset that when a dispute is resolved through arbitration, the decision will generally be *enforced* by the courts. Otherwise, arbitration would be robbed of its advantages. And, as we've already seen, it does have advantages.

Dispute resolution is typically cheaper and faster by going through arbitration than by going through the courts. It lacks the cumbersome procedures — such as extensive discovery and time-consuming, expensive motions, countermotions, and appeals — that so often bog down the judicial process.

When parties turn to arbitration, they themselves get to decide who the adjudicator will be. If they would like the dispute to be settled by someone knowledgeable about their business, they can make a point of selecting an arbitrator with the pertinent expertise. Construction disputes, for example, are commonly arbitrated by people who have experience in the construction industry. The alternative is to go before a court-assigned judge who tries all manner of cases or a jury drawn from the general population, neither of which is likely to have any kind of expertise in the relevant field. Although going before an arbitrator is usually preferable to going before a judge, it isn't always: a judge may have advantages over an arbitrator with limited experience in dispute resolution. This is a caveat you'll want to be sure to take into account when you're deciding whether to opt for arbitration and, if you do go the arbitration route, who to select as the arbitrator.

Parties that go to arbitration are in an important sense choosing for themselves what rules will govern the resolution of their disputes. In contrast, parties that turn to the judicial system have little or no say in the matter and are bound by whatever rules the courts employ. Sometimes the parties may find that using rules of their own design is best, and arbitration arrangements make it possible for them to do so. They don't usually start from scratch, however. Instead, they typically adopt rules that an arbitration association has on hand or invoke the rules of a trade association. The wide latitude that parties have in specifying rules usually works to their advantage.

Arbitration affords privacy to the parties involved in a dispute. Because the proceedings aren't a matter of public record, there's no obligation to reveal the details of the dispute and its resolution.

Because of its advantages, arbitration is assuming an increasingly important role with regard to contracts. A significant percentage of contracts are now governed by arbitration clauses. Indeed, as noted earlier, some industries rely almost entirely on arbitration, and many agreements involving international transactions make use of arbitration. So it's vitally important for you, as a lawyer, to keep its advantages clearly in mind.

8. Negotiating the Contract

We've discussed the kind of contract that you want to write for your client, but what's the best way to go about negotiating it? As you know, negotiation is a highly developed subject area, and a thorough discussion is beyond our scope. The points that we will cover here might seem obvious or intuitive. Nevertheless, they merit explicit articulation: in addition to being innately important, these principles provide a framework for approaching a negotiation methodically. And being methodical and following these principles is often very helpful.

A. Both Sides Should Understand How to Enlarge the Pie

Very often, as you know by now, a contractual term is advantageous to both parties. Sometimes, however, a term is mutually advantageous, but only one party recognizes that it would benefit both sides. Unless the second party can be convinced that the term (perhaps combined with other adjustments) works to its advantage as well as to the advantage of the first party, the two sides are likely to hit an impasse, and the term will be omitted from the contract.

Consider, for example, the term stipulating on-time performance that we looked at earlier in the Handbook. Let's assume that you're negotiating this term for your client. It's obvious to you that it —along with the price adjustment—is advantageous for the promisor as well as for your client. The promisor, on the other hand, doesn't see what its own benefit could possibly be. So you have to explain. Guaranteeing on-time performance will, you admit, cause the promisor's costs to increase by $1,000. But on-time performance is so important that your client is willing to pay, in exchange for the guarantee, an additional $2,000 to offset the promisor's additional costs. Hence, including the term along with the price adjustment in the contract benefits not only your client but the promisor as well. If you're unsuccessful in getting the promisor to understand this reasoning, the on-time performance term most likely won't appear in the contract, even though it is, in fact, mutually advantageous.

A point to keep in mind is that your client's payment to the other party for agreeing to include a term doesn't necessarily have to be monetary. Your client could, instead, pay the other party by agreeing to include terms that help the other party. Sometimes this alternative will be at least as good for your client as paying a higher price would be.

B. Be Greedy but Not Too Greedy

In addition to you and the lawyer for the other party having settled on the kind of contract to draw up — ideally, one in which all the contractual terms are mutually advantageous — the two sides need to agree on an overall price. Overall price is a crucial issue, because it determines how the contractual pie will be split up. Your goal, of course, is to obtain for your client as large a slice as possible. But you don't want to go after so large a slice — you don't want to be so greedy — as to prevent a contract from being made. In fact, if either side is too greedy, the deal will fall through, in which case there will be no contractual pie for either side to enjoy. How to go about bargaining so as to achieve your goal — obtaining a large slice of the pie for your client — and not prevent consummation of a mutually beneficial contract is discussed in the Information Theory and Bargaining appendix.

9. Suggestions for Further Reading

An excellent theoretically-informed but practical book on employee and managerial contracts is Edward P. Lazear, *Personnel Economics for Managers* (New York: John Wiley, 1998). We also recommend a number of books on contracting practice that, among other things, contain sample contracts:

James Acret, *Construction Industry Formbook*, 2nd ed. (Colorado Springs: Shepard's/McGraw-Hill, 1990).

Leslie D. Corwin and Arthur J. Ciampi, *Law Firm Partnership Agreements* (New York: Law Journal Seminars-Press, 1998).

Albert Dib, *Forms and Agreements for Architects, Engineers, and Contractors*, vol. 1, release 36 3/94. (Deerfield, Ill.: Clark Boardman Callaghan, 1994).

John F. Dolan, *Fundamentals of Commercial Activity* (Boston: Little, Brown, 1991).

George Lefcoe, *Real Estate Transactions*, 2nd ed. (Charlottesville, Va.: Michie, 1997).

Anthony Mosawi, *Entertainment Law: A Guide to Contract in the Film Industry* (London: Butterworths, 1997).

Aaron Wise and Bruce Meyer, *International Sports Law and Business*, vol. 1 (The Hague: Kluwer, 1997).

Appendix 1:
Information Theory and Bargaining

1. Moral Hazard and Incentives

We're going to examine some important topics involving situations in which a party lacks information possessed by another. This subject is relevant to many legal problems, and we will note a range of applications. Afterwards, we will turn to a specific context in which incomplete information is important, namely, bargaining.

Our first topic on information concerns a phenomenon that got its name from the insurance industry. This industry became aware quite some time ago that ownership of insurance increases the risk that insured parties will incur losses: owning insurance

---

Box 1
Moral Hazard and Information

The moral hazard problem is often considered a part of the economics of information. The reason is that the moral hazard problem of undesirable incentives in a contractual relationship is rooted in one party's lack of information about the other party's behavior – such as an insured's fire precautions or an employee's work effort. If the information can be obtained, the problem can be avoided by writing the terms of the contract accordingly.

---

tends to dull the incentive for insured parties to take actions to help prevent losses. For instance, people are naturally less concerned about property losses and thus less careful in preventing fires if they own fire insurance policies than if they don't. The insurance industry dubbed this phenomenon *moral hazard*.

The insurance example of moral hazard typifies an overarching phenomenon: after a contract is made, a party to it may have incentives to act in a way that's detrimental to the other party to the contract. For instance, an employee who's been hired may work less hard than her employer would want. Or a CEO of a corporation may make poorer decisions than its shareholders would like. Or a lawyer who has a contract to be paid by the hour may work more hours than his client would wish. Or a recipient of government welfare benefits may not try hard to find a job or to obtain good job training even though the government would want her to.

The moral hazard problem isn't just that having a contract may change the incentives of one party to the disadvantage of the other party. It's that incentives tend to be altered in a way that hurts *both* parties to the contract. To illustrate, let's consider a fire insurance example. Suppose that an insured person can very easily take a precaution — such as closing the fireplace doors when a fire is burning in the fireplace and he's leaving home (closing the doors will prevent embers from escaping into the house and setting it on fire) — and that the cost of the precautionary effort is $10 a year. Suppose, too, that if an insured person takes this precaution, the insurance company would save, on average, $100 a year (according to its actuarial tables). Taking the precaution would be in the mutual interests of the insured individual and the insurer: if the insured would bear the $10 precaution cost, the insurer could afford to reduce the insured's annual insurance premium by more than $10 — say, by $50 — given that the insurer would save $100, so both the insured and the insurer could wind up better off. But, unfortunately, the very fact that the individual is protected by insurance against fire-related losses may lead him not to take the precaution of closing the fireplace doors when he leaves home. Thus, both the insured and the insurer are worse off than they might be.

How can the moral hazard problem be solved? One possibility is for the insurer to *obtain information* about the insured's precautionary behavior. If the insurer can somehow tell whether the insured takes the precaution of closing the fireplace doors, the insurer can induce the insured to do so. For instance, the insurer could lower the annual premium only if the insured closes the fireplace doors, or the insurer could deny coverage for losses if they were caused by failure to close the fireplace doors. More generally, moral hazard problems can be cured if one party to the contract can get information about the possibly problematic behavior or situation of the other party. If an employer can tell how hard an employee is working, the employer can prevent the problem of laxity of effort by rewarding the employee for proper effort or by penalizing the employee for improper effort. If the client who has hired a lawyer on an hourly basis can figure out how many hours the legal task really requires, the client can limit in the contract the number of hours to that number. If the government can find out how hard a welfare recipient searches for a job, it can condition the continuation of benefits on the recipient's exercising proper search effort.

Solving the moral hazard problem with information is one thing. Obtaining the information is another matter. How does an insurer get information about what measures an insured takes to prevent fires? How does an employer obtain information about how hard the employee is working? How do shareholders apprise themselves of the information about business opportunities open to the CEO? How does a client determine how many hours a case ought to take the lawyer?

It depends. Sometimes obtaining information is easy. For instance, it's probably fairly easy for a fire insurer to inspect a person's home to see where smoke detectors are installed. And it's probably not too hard for an employer to find out whether an

---

Box 2
Insurance Policy Terms and Moral Hazard

Can you explain the following features of insurance policies in view of the moral hazard problem? How do they avoid moral hazard?

- If a worker is disabled, the disability insurance policy will usually limit coverage to, say, 60% of the worker's wage.
- If death is due to suicide, a life insurance policy won't pay benefits.
- If belongings stored in a basement sustain water damage because the basement floods, a homeowner's flood insurance policy won't pay.

---

employee shows up for work and puts in a full day. On the other hand, for an insurance company to determine whether an insured person really closes the fireplace doors when doing so would be appropriate or for an employer to find out whether an employee is taking too many breaks might not be easy. Likewise, ascertaining what business opportunities are available to a CEO or what number of hours is proper for a lawyer to work on a case could be a daunting task.

Difficulty in solving the moral hazard problem through acquisition of information leads to problems for the contracting parties. One problem is that, although they may solve their problem, they will have to spend money to obtain the information to do so. The insurer may be able to find out whether an insured has installed smoke detectors, but the process of finding out will require paying someone to visit the insured's premises. Another problem is that the acquired information may be fuzzy and imperfect — for example, an employer's information about how hard an employee works or a client's assessment of how many hours a case ought to take may not be very reliable. Therefore, the ability of the employer to motivate the worker properly or the client to set the appropriate number of hours for the lawyer to spend on the case might be poor.

There's a second major way in which moral hazard can be combated: through the use of an *output-based incentive* of some type, such as basing an employee's pay on the employee's contribution to profits. For instance, if the wage of a salesperson in a department store depends on his volume of sales, he'll have a natural incentive to work harder than he would if he were paid only by the hour. If the compensation of a CEO depends significantly on corporate profits, perhaps through stock options, she'll have a motive to choose business opportunities that will increase corporate profits. If an insurance policy doesn't cover losses fully — for example, because it includes a deductible feature or a ceiling on coverage — the insured party will bear part of the loss and will therefore have a reason to reduce the risk of fire. (This is an output-based incentive of a sort, in that the occurrence or nonoccurrence of a fire is an output of whether or not the insured party takes precautionary efforts.)

However, output-based incentives have a big drawback: they impose risk on people. If a CEO's pay is based in substantial part on stock options, her pay will be risky, because the amount will depend on chance elements. If an insured individual is only partially covered against loss, he will, by definition, bear some risk, but risk is exactly what he wants to avoid by purchasing insurance. As a consequence, although output-based incentives can reduce the moral hazard problem, they're often disliked because of risk imposition and are thus of limited utility. More specifically, if too much risk is imposed on a risk-averse contracting party, this party will demand higher compensation (as in the case of a CEO or an employee) or a lower price (as in the case of an insured person), and the cost to the other contracting party may be too high to be worthwhile.

Another difficulty with output-based incentives is that output may be hard to measure. For instance, determining just how much a salesperson contributes to sales may be quite difficult (perhaps one salesperson helps a customer but a different salesperson rings up the sale). Output-based incentives may be hard to fashion in such cases.

In the end, therefore, although moral hazard can be alleviated by two general methods, it typically can't be eliminated. Hence, moral hazard often remains.

A final point is that the existence of moral hazard isn't an argument for government intervention, as is sometimes mistakenly thought to be the case. If workers don't work as hard as would be best or if insured people aren't as careful to prevent loss as would be ideal, this is because the employer or the insurance company is unable to find a worthwhile way to overcome the moral hazard problem by obtaining information or using output-based incentives. Because the government doesn't typically have a superior ability to obtain information or design output-based incentives, there is no call for the government to do anything when moral hazard arises in the private sector.

2. Adverse Selection

Now we're going to turn our sights to another important phenomenon that, like the moral hazard problem, involves asymmetry of information and contracts. It's called *adverse selection*, and it arises in situations in which individuals who differ from each other in important ways selectively choose to enter into contracts.

A famous instance of adverse selection is that of used-car sales and is known as the *lemons problem*. We'd expect to find a larger proportion of cars with problems — so-called lemons — in the used-car market than in the general population of cars. The reason is that people who own lemons would be more likely to try to sell their cars than people whose cars are running well would be. Of course, we wouldn't expect all cars on the used-car market to be lemons. There are, after all, a variety of reasons for wanting to sell perfectly good cars (e.g., the owner might want to buy a new car or might decide to move to a distant city and not drive the car there).

In any case, most prospective used-car buyers will know that used cars carry a relatively high risk of being lemons. Because of this risk, the price that they'll be willing to pay for used cars will tend to be low — that is, lower than it would be if the used-car market included few, if any, lemons. The low price will often be unacceptable to potential sellers of reasonably good used cars, however, and will discourage them from putting their cars up for sale. With fewer cars in decent shape entering the used-car market than would otherwise be the case, the percentage of lemons in the market increases. Hence, the quality problem associated with used cars is exacerbated.

Ultimately, many potential mutually beneficial transactions — between sellers of good used cars and buyers willing to pay an acceptable price for them — will never occur, because the disproportion of lemons lowers the price of used cars. In other words, the tendency for lemons to be selected for sale in the used-car market adversely affects the market in that it prevents the market from functioning in a desirable way.

Adverse selection can be involved in the insurance context as well. Let's consider fire insurance again. We might expect people whose fire risks are relatively high because of the character of their property (e.g., people whose homes don't have good wiring) to be more likely than property owners in general to buy fire insurance. As a consequence, a fire insurer will receive more claims and have to charge higher premiums than it otherwise would. The higher premiums, in turn, will deter some property owners at low risk for fire from buying insurance (or lead them to buy less coverage), even though they'd be willing to pay lower premiums that the insurer would be willing to accept to cover them if it could identify them as the low-risk prospects that they are. In the end, people at high risk for fire tend to buy more insurance coverage. And this adversely affects the functioning of the insurance market by causing premiums to rise and thus leads some people at low risk to buy less coverage than otherwise.

Box 3
Can Warranties Cure Adverse Selection?

In some cases, warranties can be used to avoid the adverse selection problem. For example, a used-car dealer who knows that his cars aren't lemons could guarantee buyers that they aren't — perhaps by agreeing to pay maintenance costs for a year or to take back a car that's frequently in need of repairs. How would this sidestep the adverse selection problem?

Let's consider one more example: loans, such as bank loans to owners of new restaurants to help them get their restaurants established. We might expect bank loans to be more attractive to owners of restaurants with a lower chance of success than to owners of restaurants with a higher chance of success. The owner of a restaurant that isn't likely to be successful may view a loan as relatively cheap: if the restaurant fails and goes bankrupt, the loan won't have to be repaid. Also, if it's not particularly likely to succeed, its owners (and their friends) might be somewhat reluctant to invest a lot of their own money in the venture. What's the implication of the tendency for the owners wanting to take out loans to be those whose restaurants are more likely to go bankrupt? It means that the banks will have to charge higher interest rates so as to cover their losses when borrowers go bankrupt. But the higher interest rates discourage borrowing. This also means that owners of some promising new restaurants won't take out loans, even though banks would be willing to lend them money at lower, affordable interest rates if the banks knew these restaurant owners to be unlikely to go bankrupt and thus to be good bets. The problem in the loan market is adverse selection, in which the restaurant owners who take out loans tend to be those who are relatively less likely to repay the loans.

What can be done about adverse selection? One basic response of contracting parties who lack information is to obtain the information they need about their contracting partners. If a prospective buyer of a used car can determine its quality — for instance, by taking it to a service station for inspection — the adverse selection problem will be eliminated: lemons will be recognized as such and sell for low prices, and good used cars will be recognized as well and will sell for appropriately high prices. Therefore, someone contemplating selling a good used car will put the car on the market because he knows that he'll be able to get a fitting price for it, and a buyer who wants such a car, knowing that it isn't a lemon, will willingly pay the fitting price for it. Likewise, in the insurance example, we can imagine that the insurance company will obtain information about the fire risk of prospective policy buyers (e.g., by inspecting their houses to determine the condition of the wiring) and charge those at higher risk more for coverage. Hence, a low-risk buyer wouldn't have to pay a high premium, and the problem of adverse selection would be averted. Note that the adverse selection problem is analogous to the moral hazard problem in that both are due to an asymmetry of information and can be ameliorated in similar ways: by obtaining the appropriate necessary information.

Of course, acquiring information to prevent adverse selection is costly. Some effort is required to have a car inspected to determine whether it's a lemon, and money must be spent to ascertain which risk category a fire insurance purchaser falls into. Hence, information acquisition is, in general, an imperfect remedy for the adverse selection problem. Though it will at times substantially alleviate the problem, often it will not.

One more aspect of the adverse selection problem is that sometimes government action can help to ameliorate it. For example, consider the context of insurance where high-risk individuals cause premiums to go up and the high premiums discourage low-risk individuals from purchasing coverage. In this situation, a rule requiring all individuals to purchase coverage and to pay premiums equal to the average risk might be beneficial, but the details of why are beyond our scope.

3. Bargaining

In ending this section, we're going to take a look at bargaining — something that lawyers do all the time, of course, in making contracts, reaching settlements in litigation, and so forth. For the sake of simplicity, we'll assume that the only issue of concern in bargaining is price. The goal of a party in bargaining is to obtain as large a slice of the available "pie" as possible, but without being so aggressive in making demands that an agreement isn't reached. If either side is too greedy, the deal might fall through, and then no one will be able to enjoy any of the pie. As will become apparent in a moment, this is yet another setting in which asymmetry of information is a crucial issue.

How does a party go about bargaining so as to achieve the goal of obtaining a large slice of the pie without preventing a mutually beneficial deal from being made? One very important factor is a party's *reservation price* — the most that a buyer will pay or the least that a seller will accept. Let's use an example to illustrate the concept of reservation price and why having information about it is valuable.

Suppose that you're selling a piece of land that the prospective buyer would like to build a restaurant on. The buyer's reservation price is the maximum amount that the she'd be willing to pay for the land. This price would be determined by what the restaurant's profits are likely to be, given the location, by how much alternative sites would cost, and so forth. Suppose also that you know the buyer's exact reservation price, that it's $1,000,000. For simplicity, suppose, too, that you can credibly make a single best-and-final demand — a demand that's your only and final one. If you insist on a price that's virtually $1,000,000 — say, $999,000 — you have reason to expect that you'll get this amount.[1] The prospective

---

1. Can you think of reasons that you might not?

buyer, truly believing that you'll walk away if she refuses your demand, will rationally accept any price you demand as long as it's less than $1,000,000. You'd thus get the largest possible slice of the contractual pie, and, because your demand wouldn't exceed the buyer's reservation price, you wouldn't prevent the contract for the sale of land from being made.

In practice, of course, you won't know the other side's reservation price. And in trying to get as much as possible, you might end up asking for too much — for an amount that turns out to exceed the buyer's reservation price, which you don't know at the outset — in which case your demand will be rejected. In other words, the more you demand, the better off you'll be *if* a contract is made but the less likely a contract is to be made. As a result, you'll end up having to make a tradeoff: a higher price will result in a lower likelihood of making the contract. So your best bargaining strategy will usually be one that's less aggressive than it otherwise would be.

This issue is worth considering in greater detail, and we can do this by elaborating on the land-sale example. Suppose again, for simplicity, that you'll make one demand, a take-it-or-leave-it demand that the buyer must either accept or reject. Suppose also that, if you don't sell the land to this buyer, your next-best alternative is to sell to another buyer, one whom you know to be willing to pay $400,000. (That is, your own reservation price is $400,000.)

You must consider what the first potential buyer's reservation price might be. In contrast to the situation we looked at earlier, however, in this case you aren't certain what it is, but suppose that you do know that it is either $700,000 or $1,000,000 (the assumption that it has only two possible values is for convenience only). Suppose, too, that you know that its odds of being $700,000 are 75% and its odds of being $1,000,000 are 25%. If you demand $700,000 (or, rather, slightly below), the buyer will accept regardless of whether her valuation is $700,000 or $1,000,000, and you'll receive $700,000, $300,000 more than the $400,000 from the alternative buyer.

If you demand $1,000,000 (or, rather, slightly below) and the buyer accepts, you'll receive $1,000,000, $600,000 more than from the $400,000 alternative. But the likelihood that this will happen is only 25%. And there's a 75% probability that the buyer's valuation is $700,000, in which case she'll walk away, leaving you with no profit. So, if you ask for $1,000,000, the expected gain over the $400,000 alternative is 25% × $600,000, or $150,000. And this is less than $300,000, the amount you're certain to gain if you ask for $700,000. Hence, you should choose to demand $700,000: demanding $1,000,000 is too aggressive to be in your interest.

Sometimes, however, being tough may make sense for you. In the scenario that we just considered, for example, suppose that there's a 75% chance that the buyer's valuation is the higher amount, $1,000,000. Then insisting on $1,000,000 nets you $600,000 more than the $400,000 alternative 75% of the time. So your expected gain is 75% × $600,000, or $450,000, which is more attractive than the $300,000 gain from the $700,000 demand (unless you're very risk averse).

Having worked through a couple of versions of the land-sale scenario, what generalizations can we make about bargaining strategy?

First, when your bargaining strategy is rational, a mutually beneficial agreement won't necessarily be consummated. The reason is that it may be rational, given your knowledge, to adopt a bargaining stance that's sufficiently tough that, sometimes, the other side will reject it. This was the case in the second version of the land-sale example, the one in which the rational demand was $1,000,000. Demanding this higher amount was rational because the odds were pretty good — 75% — that the buyer placed a high valuation on the land and thus would accept the high demand. But if this turned out to be incorrect and the buyer placed a low valuation on the land, she would reject the demand.

Second, the main lessons that the land-sale scenario drives home are robust: they carry over to more complicated and realistic descriptions of the bargaining process involving, for example, multiple rounds of bargaining. Most bargaining, needless to say, consists of a series of offers and counteroffers. In such settings, as in our land-sale scenario, parties can rationally formulate the demands that they ought to make, given their uncertain knowledge of each other's situation. Sometimes deals will fall through because a party attempted to grab too large a piece of the pie and misgauged the other side's reservation price.

Third, when you're considering how to go about bargaining, you'll most likely find that the kinds of calculations we used in the example will serve you well as a benchmark. This is not to deny that bargaining is, in many respects, an art. Admittedly, there are elements of the other side's psychology that aren't easily assessed or summarized but are important in determining the result that you'll achieve. Nevertheless, you'll find that using calculations of the type illustrated in the example will help you to systematically compare different types of bargaining stances against one another.

Appendix 2:
Shopping Center Lease

Shopping Center Lease

<u>LEASE AGREEMENT</u>

THIS LEASE AGREEMENT ("Lease") dated   , by and between qq (Landlord) and yy, t/a xxy, a xx corporation (Tenant).

<u>WITNESSETH:</u>

THAT FOR AND IN CONSIDERATION of the mutual covenants and agreements herein contained, the parties hereto do hereby covenant and agree as follows:

ARTICLE I
<u>DEFINITIONS AND ATTACHMENTS</u>

Section 1.1   <u>Certain Defined Terms.</u>

As used herein, the term:

A.   "Shopping Center Area" means that certain parcel of land owned, leased or controlled by Landlord situate in the City of xx , County of xx , State of xx more-particularly described in Schedule "A-1", and upon the opening for business with the public, any such property used for expansion or anddition.

B.   "Shopping Center" means the Shopping Center Area and the andjacent parcel or parcels of land not owned, leased or controlled by Landlord but which are operated as an integral part of the shopping center known as xx, and, upon the opening for business with the public, any such property used for expansion or anddition.

C.   "Landlord's Building" means the structure or portions of a structure constructed or to be constructed by Landlord in the Shopping Center Area intended to be leased to retail tenants in the location shown on Schedule "A", as the same may be altered, reduced, expanded or replaced from time to time.

D.   "Premises" means Tenant's portion of Landlord's Building shown on Schedule "A" having the following Area:

Floor Area: xx square feet

E.   "Outsande Commencement Date" means xx

"Termination Date" means xx

F.   "Permitted Use" means the sale at retail of xx

G.   "Annual Basic Rental" means an amount equal to the product of the following figure multiplied by Tenant's Floor Area (subject to andjustment as provanded in Sections 5.1, 5.10 and 10.7: xx($xx)

H.   "Annual Percentage Rental" means a sum equal to xx percent (xx%) of the amount by which annual Gross Sales exceed the product of $xx (the "Breakpoint") multiplied by Tenant's Floor Area (subject to andjustment as provanded in Sections 5.1, 5.10 and 10.7); provanded, however, that if, during the first or last Rental Year in the Term, the Premises are not open for business with the general public for twelve (12) full calendar months, the Breakpoint shall be andjusted for any such Rental Year by multiplying the Breakpoint specified above by a fraction, the numerator of which shall be the actual number of full calendar months in such Rental Year during which the Premises were open for business with the general public, and the denominator of which shall be twelve (12).

I.   "Aâdvance Rental" means the sum of $xx. See Section 5.9.

J.   "HVAC Equipment Contribution Rate" means the sum of $xx. See Schedule F.

K.   "Mall Heating, Ventilating and Air-Conditioning Equipment Contribution Rate" means the sum of $xx. See Section 10.6.

L.   "Promotion Fund Contribution Rate" means the sum of $xx. See Section 11.2.

        "Andvertising Participation Fund Rate" means the sum of $xx. See Section 11.2.B.

        "Merchants' Association Contribution Rate" means the sum of $xx. See Section 11.2.

        "Andvertising Participation Fund Rate" means the sum of $xx. See Section 11.9.B.

M.   "Sprinkler Contribution Rate" means the sum of $xx.
See Section 12.3.

N.   "Trash Removal Service Charge" means the sum of $xx.
See Section 8.4.

O.   "Water and Sewer Charge" means the sum of $xx.
See Schedule E.

P.   "Tenant Notice Anddress" means

     yy
     xx

Q.   "Tenant Trade Name" means xxy

which Tenant represents it is entitled to use pursuant to all applicable laws.

R.   "Store Hours" means xx.

S.   "Restriction Area" means that geographic area within a randius of xx miles measured from the Premises.

T.   "Landlord's Floor Area" means the aggregate number of square feet of Landlord's leasable floor area in Landlord's Building (exclusive of Anchor Stores and exclusive of any building not structurally connected to the enclosed mall or not having an opening into the enclosed mall) which, with respect to any such floor area which has been leased to any rent-paying tenant, shall be determined in accordance with the provisions of any lease applicable thereto and which, with respect to any such floor area not so leased, shall consist of all such leasable floor area in Landlord's Building designed for the exclusive use and occupancy of rent-paying tenants, which shall exclude Common Areas, storage areas leased separately from retail areas, mezzanine areas and areas used for Landlord's management and promotion offices.

U.   "Tenant's Floor Area" means the number of square feet contained in that portion of Landlord's Floor Area constituting the Premises which shall be measured (a) with respect to the front and rear wandth thereof, from the exterior face of the andjacent exterior or corrandor wall or, if none, from the center of the demising partition, to the opposite exterior face of the andjacent exterior or corrandor wall or, if none, to the center of the opposite demising partition, and (b) with respect to the depth thereof, from the front lease line to the exterior face of the rear exterior walls or corrandor wall, or, if neither, to the center of the rear demising partition; and in no case shall there be any deduction for columns or other structural elements within any tenant's premises.

V.   "Common Areas" means those areas and facilities which may be furnished by Landlord or others in or near the Shopping Center Area for the non-exclusive general common use of tenants, Anchor Stores and other occupants of the Shopping Center, their officers, agents, employees and customers, including (without limitation) parking areas, access areas (other than public streets), employee parking areas, truckways, driveways, loanding docks and areas, delivery passageways, package pick-up stations, sandewalks, interior and exterior pedestrian walkways and pedestrian brandges, malls, promenandes, mezzanines, roofs, sprinklers, plazas, courts, ramps, common seating areas, landscaped and planted areas, retaining walls, balconies, stairways, escalators, elevators, bus stops, first-aand stations, sewage treatment facilities (if any) lighting facilities, comfort stations or rest rooms, civic center, meeting rooms, and other similar areas, facilities or improvements.

W. "Default Rate" means an annual rate of interest equal to the lesser of (i) the maximum rate of interest for which Tenant may lawfully contract in the State in which the Shopping Center is situate, or (ii) eighteen percent (18%).

X. "Anchor Store" means any department or specialty store which either (i) occupies a floor area in excess of 50,000 square feet in the Shopping Center, or (ii) is designated an Anchor Store in a notice to that effect given by Landlord to Tenant.

Y. "Landlord's Leased Floor Area" means the monthly average of the aggregate number of square feet contained in those portions of Landlord's Floor Area leased to tenants (including the Premises) as of the first day of each calendar month during the billing period in question, but not less than eighty-five percent (85%) of Landlord's Floor Area.

Section 1.2. A<u>dditional Defined Terms.</u>

The following andditional terms are defined in the Sections of this Lease noted below:

Term	Section
"Andditional Rental"	5.1
"Annual Merchants' Association Contribution"	11.2
"Association"	11.1
"Association Year"	11.4
"Casualty"	14.1
"Commencement Date"	3.1
"Consumer Price Index"	11.2
"Electricity Component"	Schedule E (if applicable)
"Electricity Factor"	Schedule E (if applicable)
"Event of Default"	17.1
"Expansion Opening Contribution"	11.2
"First Association Year"	11.4
"Fiscal Year"	Schedule F (if applicable)
"Gross Sales"	5.5
"Hazardous Substance"	8.6
"HVAC Equipment Contribution"	Schedule F (if applicable)
"HVAC Factor"	Schedule F (if applicable)
"Landlord's Improvement Costs"	10.7
"Landlord's Operating Costs"	10.5
"Liquandated Damages"	17.3
"Mortgage"	18.2
"Mortgagee"	18.2
"Release"	8.6
"Rental"	5.1
"Rental Year"	5.4
"Taxes	6.1
"Tax Year	6.3
"Tenant's Electrical Installation"	Schedule E (if applicable)

"Tenant's HVAC Charge"	Schedule F (if applicable)
"Tenant's V/CW Charge"	Schedule E (if applicable)
"Term"	3.1
"Termination Damages	17.3
"Umpire"	Schedule E (if applicable)
"V/CW Equipment Contribution"	Schedule F (if applicable)
"V/CW Factor"	Schedule F (if applicable)

Section 1.3. Attachments.

The following documents are attached hereto, and such documents, as well as all drawings and documents prepared pursuant thereto, shall be deemed to be a part hereof:

Schedule "A"	-	Drawing of Shopping Center Area including Landlord's Building and Tenant's Premises
Schedule "A-1"	-	Legal Description of Shopping Center Area
Schedule "A-2"	-	Legal Description of Shopping Center
Schedule "B"	-	None
Schedule "C"	-	None
Schedule "D"	-	None
Schedule "E"	-	Utility Consumption and Payment Schedule
Schedule "F"	-	Tenant Heating, Ventilating and Air-Conditioning Schedule

ARTICLE II
PREMISES

Section 2.1. Demise.

Landlord hereby leases to Tenant, and Tenant hereby rents from Landlord, the Premises having the Floor Area as set forth in clause D of Section 1.1. hereof, which Landlord and Tenant hereby conclusively agree represents Tenant's Floor Area for all purposes of this Lease.

Landlord warrants that it and no other person or corporation has the right to lease the Premises hereby demised, and that so long as Tenant is not in default hereunder, Tenant shall have peaceful and quiet use and possession of the Premises, subject to any Mortgage, and all matters of record or other agreements to which this Lease is or may hereafter be subordinated.

Notwithstanding anything to the contrary contained herein, the Premises have been inspected by Tenant who shall be deemed to have accepted the same as existing as of the date Landlord delivers the Premises to Tenant for completion of all work required of it.

ARTICLE III
TERM

Section 3.1. Term.

The term of this Lease (the "Term") shall commence on that date (the "Commencement Date") which shall be the earlier to occur of (a) the Outsaide Commencement Date or (b) the opening by Tenant of its business in the Premises, and shall terminate on the Termination Date. Landlord and Tenant agree, upon demand of the other, to execute a declaration setting forth the Commencement Date as soon as the Commencement Date has been determined.

Section 3.2. Termination.

This Lease shall terminate on the Termination Date, without the necessity of any notice from either Landlord or Tenant to terminate the same, and Tenant hereby waives notice to vacate or quit the Premises and agrees that Landlord shall be entitled to the benefit of all provisions of law respecting the summary recovery of possession of the Premises from a tenant holding over to the same extent as if statutory notice hand been given. Tenant hereby agrees that if it fails to Surrender the Premises at the end of the Term, or any renewal thereof, Tenant will be liable to Landlord for any and all damages which Landlord shall suffer by reason thereof, and Tenant will indemnify Landlord against all claims and demands mande by any succeeding tenants against Landlord, founded upon delay by Landlord in delivering possession of the Premises to such succeeding tenant. For the period of three (3) months prior to the expiration of the Term, Landlord shall have the right to display on the exterior of the Premises a "For Rent" sign (not to exceed one foot by one foot in size) and during such period Landlord may show the Premises and all parts thereof to prospective tenants during normal business hours.

Section 3.3. Holding Over.

If Tenant shall be in possession of the Premises after the expiration of the Term, in the absence of any agreement extending the Term, the tenancy under this Lease shall become one from month to month, terminable by either party on thirty (30) days' prior notice, and shall be subject to all of the terms and conditions of this Lease as though the Term hand been extended from month to month, except that (i) the Annual Basic Rental payable hereunder for each month during saand holdover period shall be equal to twice the monthly installment of Annual Basic Rental payable during the last month of the Term, (ii) the installments of Annual Percentage Rental payable hereunder for each such month shall be equal to one-twelfth (1/12th) of the average Annual Percentage Rental payable hereunder for the last three (3) Rental Years of the Term, or if the Term is less than three (3) Rental Years, then such installments shall be equal to one-twelfth (1/12th) of the Annual Percentage Rental payable hereunder for the last complete Rental Year preceding expiration of the Term, and (iii) all Andditional Rental payable hereunder shall be prorated for each month during such holdover period.

ARTICLE IV
USE

Section 4.1. Prompt Occupancy and Use.

Tenant shall occupy the Premises upon commencement of the Term and thereafter will continuously use the Premises for the Permitted Use and for no other purpose whatsoever.

Section 4.2. Storage and Office Areas.

Tenant shall use only such minor portions of the Premises for storage and office purposes as are reasonably required therefor.

Section 4.3. Tenant Trade Name.

Unless otherwise approved by Landlord, Tenant shall conduct business in the Premises only in the Tenant Trade Name.

Section 4.4. Store Hours.

Tenant shall cause its business to be conducted and operated in good faith and in such manner as shall assure the transaction of a maximum volume of business in and at the Premises. Tenant covenants and agrees that the Premises shall remain open for business at least during the Store Hours or such other hours as shall be seasonally andjusted by Landlord. If Tenant shall fail to cause its business to be operated during the hours required by the preceding sentence, or as otherwise required by Landlord, in anddition to any other remedy available to Landlord under this Lease, Tenant shall pay to Landlord, as liquandated damages for such breach, a sum equal to One Hundred Dollars ($100.00) for each hour or portion thereof during which Tenant shall fail to so operate.

If Tenant shall request Landlord's approval of the opening of the Premises for business for periods exceeding those designated above and Landlord shall approve such request, Tenant shall pay for any andditional costs incurred by Landlord in connection with Tenant's opening the Premises for business during such andditional hours, including but not limited to, a proportionate share of any andditional amounts of Landlord's Operating Costs, andditional costs of heating, ventilating and air-conditioning the Premises, and andditional utilities furnished to the Premises by Landlord.

ARTICLE V
RENTAL

Section 5.1. Rentals Payable.

Tenant covenants and agrees to pay to Landlord as rental ("Rental") for the Premises, the following:

(a)   the Annual Basic Rental specified in clause G of Section 1.1; plus
(b)   the Annual Percentage Rental specified in clause II of Section 1.1; plus
(c)   all andditional sums, charges or amounts of whatever nature to be paand by Tenant to Landlord in accordance with the provisions of this Lease, whether

or not such sums, charges or amounts are referred to as andditional rental (collectively referred to as "Andditional Rental");

provanded, however, that the Annual Basic Rental and the minimum amount of Gross Sales utilized in the computation of Annual Percentage Rental shall be andjusted proportionately for any Rental Year of more or less than twelve (12) calendar months.

Section 5.2. Annual Basic Rental.

Annual Basic Rental shall be payable in equal monthly installments in andvance on the first day of each full calendar month during the Term, the first such payment to include also any prorated Annual Basic Rental for the period from the date of the commencement of the Term to the first day of the first full calendar month in the Term.

Section 5.3. Annual Percentage Rental.

Annual Percentage Rental shall be determined and payable monthly on or before the fifteenth (15th) day following the close of each full calendar month during the Term, based on Gross Sales for the preceding calendar month. Monthly payments of Annual Percentage Rental shall be calculated by (a) divanding the product specified in clause H of Section 1.1. by twelve (12); (b) subtracting the quotient thus obtained from the amount of Gross Sales for the month in question, and (c) multiplying the difference thus obtained (if greater than zero) by the percentage specified in clause II of Section 1.1. The first monthly payment of Annual Percentage Rental due hereunder shall include prorated Annual Percentage Rental based on Gross Sales from the Commencement Date through the last day of the month immediately prior to the first full calendar month in the Term. As soon as practicable after the end of each Rental Year the Annual Percentage Rental paand or payable for such Rental Year shall be andjusted between Landlord and Tenant, and each party hereby agrees to pay to the other, on demand, the amount of any excess or deficiency in Annual Percentage Rental paand by Tenant to Landlord during the preceding Rental Year as may be necessary to effect andjustment to the agreed Annual Percentage Rental.

Section 5.4. "Rental Year" Defined.

The first "Rental Year" shall commence on the first day of the Term and shall end at the close of the twelfth full calendar month following the commencement of the Term; thereafter each Rental Year shall consist of successive periods of twelve calendar months. Any portion of the Term remaining at the end of the last full Rental Year shall constitute the final Rental Year and all Rental shall be apportioned therefor.

Section 5.5. "Gross Sales" Defined.

"Gross Sales" means the actual sales prices or rentals of all goods, wares and merchandise sold, leased, licensed or delivered and the actual charges for all services performed by Tenant or by any subtenant, licensee or concessionaire in, at, from, or arising out of the use of the Premises, whether for wholesale, retail, cash, credit, trande-in or otherwise, without reserve or deduction for inability or failure to collect. Gross Sales shall include, without limitation, sales and services (a) where the orders therefor originate in, at, from, or arising out of the use of the Premises, whether delivery or performance is mande from the Premises or from some other place, (b) mande or performed by mail, telephone, or telegraph orders, (c) mande or performed by means of mechanical or other vending devices in the Premises, or (d) which Tenant or any subtenant, licensee, concessionaire or other person in the normal and customary course of its business would credit or attribute to its operations in any part of the Premises. Any deposit not refunded shall be included in Gross Sales. Each installment or credit sale shall be treated as a sale for the full price in the month during which such sale is mande, regardless of whether or when Tenant receives payment therefor. No franchise, occupancy or capital stock tax and no income or similar tax based on income or profits shall be deducted from Gross Sales.

The following shall not be included in Gross Sales: (i) any exchange of merchandise between stores of Tenant where such exchange is mande solely for the convenient operation of Tenant's business and not for the purpose of consummating a sale mande in, at or from the Premises, or for the purpose of depriving Landlord of the benefit of a sale which would otherwise be mande in or at the Premises, (ii) returns to shippers or manufacturers, (iii) cash or credit refunds to customers on transactions (not to exceed the actual selling price of the item returned) otherwise included in Gross Sales, (iv) sales of trande fixtures, machinery and equipment after use thereof in the conduct of Tenant's business, (v) amounts collected and paand by Tenant to any government for any sales or excise tax, and (vi) the amount of any discount on sales to employees.

Section 5.6. Statements of Gross Sales.

Tenant shall deliver to Landlord: (a) within ten (10) days after the close of each calendar month of the Term, a written report signed by Tenant or by an authorized officer or agent of Tenant, showing the Gross Sales mande in the preceding calendar month and (b) within sixty (60) days after the close of each Rental Year, a statement of Gross Sales for the preceding Rental Year which shall conform to and be in accordance with generally accepted accounting principles and Section 5.5. The annual statement shall be accompanied by the signed certificate of an independent Certified Public Accountant stating specifically that (i) he has examined the report of Gross Sales for the preceding Rental Year, (ii) his examination included such tests of Tenant's books and records as he consandered necessary or appropriate under the circumstances, (iii) such report presents fairly the Gross Sales of the preceding Rental Year, and (iv) the saand Gross Sales conform with and are computed in compliance with the definition of Gross Sales contained in Section 5.5 hereof. If Tenant shall fail to deliver such annual statement and certificate to Landlord within saand sixty (60) day period, Landlord shall have the right thereafter to employ an independent Certified Public Accountant to examine such books and records, including without limitation all records required by Section 5.7, as may be necessary to certify the amount of Tenant's Gross Sales for such Rental Year, and Tenant shall pay to Landlord the cost thereof as Andditional Rental.

If such audit shall disclose that Tenant's records, in the opinion of such independent Certified Public Accountant, are inandequate to disclose such Gross Sales, Landlord shall be entitled to collect, as Andditional Rental, an equitable sum determined by such independent Certified Public Accountant but not exceeding fifty percent (50%) of the Annual Basic Rental payable by Tenant during the period in question.

Section 5.7. Tenant's Records.

For the purpose of permitting verification by Landlord of any amounts due as Rental, Tenant will (i) cause the business upon the Premises to be operated so that a duplicate sales slip, invoice or non-resetable cash register receipt, serially numbered, or such other device for recording sales as Landlord approves, shall be issued with each sale or transaction, whether for cash, credit or exchange, and (ii) preserve for a least three (3) years, and during the Term shall keep at the Tenant Notice Anddress or the Premises, a general ledger, required receipts and disbursement journals and such sales records and other supporting documentation, together with original or duplicate books and records, which shall disclose all information required to determine Tenant's Gross Sales and which shall conform to and be in accordance with generally accepted accounting principles. At any time or from time to time after andvance notice to Tenant, Landlord or any Mortgagee, their agents and accountants, shall have the right during business hours to make any examination or audit of such books and records which Landlord or such Mortgagee may desire. If such audit shall disclose a liability in any Rental Year for Rental in excess of the Rental theretofore paand by Tenant for such period, Tenant shall promptly pay such liability. Should any such liability for Rental equal or exceed three percent (3%) of Annual Percentage Rental previously paand for such Rental Year, or if such audit shall disclose that Tenant has underreported Gross Sales by five percent (5%) or more during any Rental Year, (a) Tenant shall promptly pay the cost of audit and interest at the Default Rate on all andditional Annual Percentage Rental then payable, accounting from the date such andditional Annual Percentage Rental was due and payable, and (b) an Event of Default shall be deemed to exist unless, within ten (10) days after Landlord shall have given Tenant notice of such liability, Tenant shall furnish Landlord with evandence satisfactorily demonstrating to Landlord that such liability for andditional Annual Percentage Rental was the result of good faith error on Tenant's part. If such audit shall disclose that Tenant's records, in Landlord's opinion, are inandequate to accurately reflect Tenant's Gross Sales, Landlord shall have the right to retain a consultant to prepare and establish a proper recording system for the determination of Tenant's Gross Sales and Tenant agrees that it shall use the system, books and records prescribed by such consultant for such purpose. Tenant shall pay to Landlord, as Andditional Rental, the fees and expenses of such consultant.

Section 5.8. Payment of Rental.

Tenant shall pay all Rental when due and payable, without any setoff, deduction or prior demand therefor whatsoever. Except as provanded herein, Tenant shall not pay any Rental earlier than one (1) month in andvance of the date on which it is due. If Tenant shall fail to pay any Rental within seven (7) days after the same is due, Tenant shall be obligated to pay a late payment charge equal to the greater of One Hundred Dollars ($100.00) or ten percent (10%) of any Rental payment not paand when due to reimburse Landlord for its andditional andministrative costs. In anddition, any Rental which is not paand within seven (7) days after the same is due shall bear interest at the Default Rate from the first day due until paand. Any Andditional Rental which shall become due shall be payable, unless otherwise provanded herein, with the next installment of Annual Basic Rental. Rental and statements required of Tenant shall be paand and delivered to Landlord at the management office of Landlord in the Shopping Center Area during normal business hours, or at such other place as Landlord may from time to time designate in a notice to Tenant. Any payment by Tenant or acceptance by Landlord of a lesser amount than shall be due from Tenant to Landlord shall be treated as a payment on account. The acceptance by Landlord or a check for a lesser amount with an endorsement or statement thereon, or upon any letter accompanying such check, that such lesser amount is payment in full, shall be given no effect, and Landlord may accept such check without prejudice to any other rights or remedies which Landlord may have against Tenant.

Section 5.9. Andvance Rental.

Upon execution of this Lease by Tenant, Tenant shall pay to Landlord the Andvance Rental, the same to be held as security for the performance by Tenant of all obligations imposed under this Lease which Tenant is required to perform prior to the commencement of the Term. If

Tenant shall faithfully perform all such obligations, then the Andvance Rental shall be applied, pro tanto, by Landlord against the Rental first becoming due hereunder. Otherwise, Landlord shall be entitled to apply the Andvance Rental, pro tanto, against any damages which it may sustain by reason of Tenant's failure to perform its obligations under this Lease, but such application shall not preclude Landlord from recovering greater damages if the same can be established.

Section 5.10. Future Expansion.

In the event that during the Term (i) andditional Anchor Stores are constructed in the Shopping Center and Landlord's Floor Area is not diminished by more than [10,000] square feet as a result thereof, or (ii) one or more expansions of Landlord's Building, each involving the anddition of at least 50,000 square feet of Landlord's Floor Area, are constructed, then, upon the opening for business of each such andditional Anchor Store or expansion of Landlord's Building, the Annual Basic Rental shall be increased by ten percent (10%) for each such Anchor Store or expansion opening and the Breakpoint shall be increased by a like percentage.

＊　　＊　　＊

ARTICLE VIII
OPERATIONS

Section 8.1. Operations by Tenant.

In regard to the use and occupancy of the Premises, Tenant will at its expense: (a) keep the insande and outsande of all glass in the doors and windows of the Premises clean; (b) keep all exterior store surfaces of the Premises clean; (c) replace promptly any cracked or broken glass of the Premises with glass of like color, grande and quality; (d) maintain the Premises in a clean, orderly and sanitary condition and free of insects, rodents, vermin and other pests; (e) keep any garbage, trash, rubbish or other refuse in rat-proof containers within the interior of the Premises until removed; (f) deposit such garbage, trash, rubbish and refuse, on a daily basis, in designated receptacles provanded by Landlord; (g) keep all mechanical apparatus free of vibration and noise which may be transmitted beyond the Premises; (h) comply with all laws, ordinances, rules and regulations of governmental authorities and all reasonable recommendations of Landlord's casualty insurer(s) and other applicable insurance rating organization now or hereafter in effect; (i) light the show windows of the Premises and exterior signs and turn the same on to the extent required by Landlord; (j) keep in the Premises and maintain in good working order one (1) or more type 2A lOBC dry chemical fire extinguisher(s); (k) comply with and observe all rules and regulations established by Landlord from time to time which apply generally to all retail tenants in the Shopping Center Area; (l) maintain sufficient and seasonal inventory and have sufficient number of personnel to maximize sales volume in the Premises; and (m) conduct its business in all respects in a dignified manner in accordance with high standards of store operation consistent with the quality of operation of the Shopping Center Area as determined by Landlord and provande an appropriate mercantile quality comparable with the entire Shopping Center.

In regard to the use and occupancy of the Premises and the Common Areas, Tenant will not: (n) place or maintain any merchandise, signage, trash, refuse or other articles in any vestibule or entry of the Premises, on the footwalks or corrandors andjacent thereto or elsewhere on the exterior of the Premises, nor obstruct any driveway, corrandor, footwalk, parking area, mall or any other Common Areas; (o) use or permit the use of any objectionable andvertising medium such as, without limitation, loudspeakers, phonographs, public anddress systems, sound amplifiers, reception of randio or television broandcasts within the Shopping Center, which is in any manner audible or visible-outsande of the Premises; (p) permit undue accumulations of or bum garbage, trash, rubbish or other refuse within or without the Premises; (q) cause or permit objectionable odors (in Landlord's opinion) to emanate or to be dispelled from the Premises; (r) solicit business in any Common Areas; (s) distribute handbills or other andvertising matter in any Common Areas (including placing any of the same in or upon any automobiles parked in the parking areas); (t) permit the parking of vehicles so as to interfere with the use of any driveway, corrandor, footwalk, parking area, mall or other Common Areas; (u) receive or ship articles of any kind outsande the designated loanding areas for the Premises; (v) use the mall, corrandor or any other Common Areas andjacent to the Premises for the sale or display of any merchandise or for any other business, occupation or undertaking; (w) conduct or permit to be conducted any auction, fictitious fire sale, going out of business sale, bankruptcy sale (unless directed by court order), or other similar type sale in or connected with the Premises (but this provision shall not restrict the absolute freedom of Tenant in determining its own selling prices, nor shall it preclude the conduct of periodic seasonal, promotional or clearance sales); (x) use or permit the use of any portion of the Premises in a manner which will be in violation of law, or for any activity of a type which is not generally consandered appropriate for regional shopping centers conducted in accordance with good and generally accepted standards of operation; (y) place a loand upon any floor which exceeds the floor loand which the floor was designed to carry; (z) operate its heating or air-conditioning in such a manner as to drain heat or air-conditioning from the Common Areas or from the premises of any other tenant or other occupant of the Shopping Center; or (aa) use the Premises for any unlawful or illegal business, use or purpose, or for any business, use or purpose which is immoral or disreputable (including without limitation "andult entertainment establishments" and "andult bookstores"), or which is hazardous, or in such manner as to constitute a nuisance of any kind (public or private), or for any purpose or in any way in violation of the certificates of occupancy (or other similar approvals of applicable governmental authorities).

Tenant acknowledges that it is Landlord's intent that the Shopping Center Area be operated in a manner which is consistent with the highest standards of decency and morals prevailing in the community which it serves. Toward that end, Tenant agrees that it will not sell, distribute, display or offer for sale any item which, in Landlord's good faith judgment, is inconsistent with the quality of operation of the Shopping Center Area or may tend to injure or detract from the moral character or image of the Shopping Center Area within such community. Without limiting the generality of the foregoing, Tenant will not sell, distribute, display or offer for sale (i) any roach clip, water pipe, bong, coke spoon, cigarette papers, hypodermic syringe or other paraphernalia commonly used in the use or ingestion of illicit drugs, (ii) any pornographic, lewd, suggestive, or "andult" newspaper, book, magazine, film, picture recording, representation or merchandise of any kind, or (iii) any handgun.

Section 8.2. Signs and Andvertising.

Tenant will not place or suffer to be placed or maintained on the exterior of the Premises, or any part of the interior visible from the exterior thereof, any sign, banner, andvertising matter or any other thing of any kind (including, without limitation, any hand-lettered andvertising), and will not place or maintain any decoration, letter or andvertising matter on the glass of any window or door of the Premises without first obtaining Landlord's approval. Tenant will, at its sole cost and expense, maintain such sign, banner, decoration, lettering, andvertising matter or other thing as may be permitted hereunder in good condition and repair at all times.

Section 8.3. Painting and Displays by Tenant.

Tenant will not paint or decorate any part of the exterior of the Premises, or any part of the interior of the Premises visible from the exterior thereof, without first obtaining Landlord's approval. Tenant will install and maintain at all times, subject to the other provisions of this Section, displays of merchandise in the show windows (if any) of the Premises. All articles, and the arrangement, style, color and general appearance thereof, in the interior of the Premises including, without limitation, window displays, andvertising matter, signs, merchandise and store fixtures, shall be in keeping with the character and standards of the improvements within the Shopping Center, as determined by Landlord. Landlord reserves the right to require Tenant to correct any non-conformity.

Section 8.4. Trash Removal Service.

At its option, Landlord may furnish (or authorize others to furnish) a service for the removal of trash from receptacles designated by Landlord for the daily deposit by Tenant of its garbage, trash, rubbish or other refuse, and, if it shall do so, then in each Rental Year, at Landlord's election, Tenant shall either (i) reimburse Landlord monthly, as Andditional Rental, for all costs incurred by Landlord in furnishing such service, or (ii) pay Landlord the Trash Removal Service Charge, if any, set forth in clause N of Section 1.1. in twelve (12) equal monthly installments, subject to andjustments reflecting any increase in Landlord's cost and expense in furnishing such trash removal service, or (iii) pay directly such person, firm or corporation authorized by Landlord to pròvande such trash removal service; provanded, however, that all amounts which Tenant is obligated to pay to Landlord pursuant to clause (i) or (ii) above shall not exceed the amounts which Tenant would otherwise be obligated to pay directly to the same independent contractor utilized by Landlord for the removal of Tenant's trash, if Tenant were dealing with such contractor at arm's length for trash removal services for the Premises.

Section 8.5. Permitted Use Disclaimer.

Nothing contained in this Lease shall be construed to indicate any intent or attempt on the part of Landlord to restrict the price or prices at which Tenant may sell any goods or services permitted to be sold at or from the Premises pursuant to this Lease.

Section 8.6. Hazardous Substances.

Tenant shall not use or allow the Premises to be used for the Release, storage, use, treatment, disposal or other handling of any Hazardous Substance, without the prior consent of Landlord. The term "Release" shall have the same meaning as is ascribed to it in the Comprehensive Environmental Response Compensation and Liability Act, 42 U.S.C. § 9601 et seq., as amended,

("CERCLA"). The term "Hazardous Substance" means (i) any substance defined as a "hazardous substance" under CERCLA, (ii) petroleum, petroleum products, natural gas, natural gas liquands, liquefied natural gas, and synthetic gas, and (iii) any other substance or material deemed to be hazardous, dangerous, toxic, or a pollutant under any federal, state or local law, code, ordinance or regulation.

Tenant shall: (a) give prior notice to Landlord of any activity or operation to be conducted by Tenant at the Premises which involves the Release, use, handling, generation, treatment, storage, or disposal of any Hazardous Substance ("Tenant's Hazardous Substance Activity"), (b) comply with all federal, state, and local laws, codes, ordinances, regulations, permits and licensing conditions governing the Release, discharge, emission, or disposal of any Hazardous Substance and prescribing methods for or other limitations on storing, handling, or otherwise managing Hazardous Substances, (c) at its own expense, promptly contain and remediate any Release of Hazardous Substances arising from or related to Tenant's Hazardous Substance Activity in the Premises, Landlord's Building, the Shopping Center, the Shopping Center Area or the environment and remediate and pay for any resultant damage to property, persons, and/or the environment, (d) give prompt notice to Landlord, and all appropriate regulatory authorities, of any Release of any Hazardous Substance in the Premises, Landlord's Building, the Shopping Center, the Shopping Center Area or the environment arising from or related to Tenant's Hazardous Substance Activity, which Release is not mande pursuant to and in conformance with the terms of any permit or license duly issued by appropriate governmental authorities, any such notice to include a description of measures taken or proposed to be taken by Tenant to contain and remediate the Release and any resultant damage to property, persons, or the environment, (e) at Landlord's request, which shall not be more frequent than once per calendar year, retain an independent engineer or other qualified consultant or expert acceptable to Landlord, to conduct, at Tenant's expense, an environmental audit of the Premises and immediate surrounding areas, and the scope of work to be performed by such engineer, consultant, or expert shall be approved in andvance by Landlord, and all of the engineer's, consultant's, or expert's work product shall be mande available to Landlord, (f) at Landlord's request from time to time, execute affandavits, representations and the like concerning Tenant's best knowledge and belief regarding the presence of Hazardous Substances in the Premises, (g) reimburse to Landlord, upon demand, the reasonable cost of any testing for the purpose of ascertaining if there has been any Release of Hazardous Substances in the Premises, if such testing is required by any governmental agency or Landlord's Mortgagee, (h) upon expiration or termination of this Lease, surrender the Premises to Landlord free from the presence and contamination of any Hazardous Substance.

ARTICLE IX
REPAIRS AND ALTERATIONS

Section 9.1. Repairs To Be Mande By Landlord.

Landlord, at its expense, will make, or cause to be mande structural repairs to exterior walls, structural columns, roof penetrations and structural floors which collectively enclose the Premises (excluding, however, all doors, door frames, storefronts, windows and glass); provanded Tenant shall give Landlord notice of the necessity for such repairs.

Section 9.2. <u>Repairs To Be Mande By Tenant</u>.

All repairs to the Premises or any installations, equipment or facilities therein, other than those repairs required to be mande by Landlord pursuant to Sections 9.1, 12.3 or Section 14.1, shall be mande by Tenant at its expense. Without limiting the generality of the foregoing, Tenant will keep the interior of the Premises, together with all electrical, plumbing and other mechanical installations therein and (if and to the extent provanded in Schedule F) the heating, ventilating and air conditioning system installed by Tenant in the Premises, in good order and repair and will make all replacements from time to time required thereto at its expense. Tenant will surrender the Premises at the expiration of the Term or at such other time as it may vacate the Premises in as good condition as when received, excepting depreciation caused by ordinary wear and tear, damage by Casualty, unavoandable accandent or Act of God. Tenant will not overloand the electrical wiring serving the Premises or within the Premises, and will install at its expense, subject to the provisions of Section 9.4, any andditional electrical wiring which may be required in connection with Tenant's apparatus. Any damage or injury sustained by any person because of mechanical, electrical, plumbing or any other equipment or installations, whose maintenance and repair shall be the responsibility of Tenant, shall be paand for by Tenant, and Tenant hereby agrees to indemnify and hold Landlord harmless from and against all claims, actions, damages and liability in connection therewith, including, but not limited to attorneys' and other professional fees, and any other cost which Landlord might reasonably incur.

Section 9.3. <u>Damage to Premises</u>.

Tenant will repair promptly at its expense any damage to the Premises and, upon demand, shall reimburse Landlord (as Andditional Rental) for the cost of the repair of any damage elsewhere in the Shopping Center, caused by or arising from the installation or removal of property in or from the Premises, regardless of fault or by whom such damage shall be caused (unless caused by Landlord, its agents, employees or contractors). If Tenant shall fail to commence such repairs within five (5) days after notice to do so from Landlord, Landlord may make or cause the same to be mande and Tenant agrees to pay to Landlord promptly upon Landlord's demand, as Andditional Rental, the cost thereof with interest thereon at the Default Rate until paand.

Section 9.4. <u>Alterations by Tenant</u>.

Tenant will not make any alterations, renovations, improvements or other installations in, on or to any part of the Premises (including, without limitation, any alterations of the storefront, signs, structural alterations, or any cutting or drilling into any part of the Premises or any securing of any fixture, apparatus, or equipment of any kind to any part of the Premises) unless and until Tenant shall have caused plans and specifications therefor to have been prepared, at Tenant's expense, by an architect or other duly qualified person and shall have obtained Landlord's approval thereof. If such approval is granted, Tenant shall cause the work described in such plans and specifications to be performed, at its expense, promptly, efficiently, competently and in a good and workmanlike manner by duly qualified and licensed persons or entities, using first grande materials, without interference with or disruption to the operations of tenants or other occupants of the Shopping Center. All such work shall comply with all applicable codes, rules, regulations and ordinances.

Section 9.5. Changes and Andditions to Shopping Center.

Landlord reserves the right at any time and from time to time to (a) make or permit changes or revisions in the plan for the Shopping Center or the Shopping Center Area including andditions to, subtractions from, rearrangements of, alterations of, modifications of, or supplements to, the building areas, walkways, driveways, parking areas, or other Common Areas, (b) construct improvements in Landlord's Building and the Shopping Center Area and to make alterations thereof or andditions thereto and to build anddivisional stories on or in any such building(s) and build andjoining same, including (without limitation) kiosks, pushcarts and other displays in the Common Areas, and (c) make or permit changes or revisions in the Shopping Center or the Shopping Center Area, including andditions thereto, and to convey portions of the Shopping Center Area to others for the purpose of constructing thereon other buildings or improvements, including andditions thereto and alterations thereof; provanded, however, that no such changes, rearrangements or other construction shall reduce the parking areas below the number of parking spaces required by law.

Section 9.6. Roof and Walls.

Landlord shall have the exclusive right to use all or any part of the roof of the Premises for any purpose; to erect anddivisional stories or other structures over all or any part of the Premises; to erect in connection with the construction thereof temporary scaffolds and other aands to construction on the exterior of the Premises, provanded that access to the Premises shall not be denied; and to install, maintain, use, repair and replace within the Premises pipes, ducts, conduits, wires and all other mechanical equipment serving other parts of the Shopping Center Area, the same to be in locations within the Premises as will not unreasonably deny Tenant's use thereof. Landlord may make any use it desires of the sande or rear walls of the Premises or other structural elements of the Premises (including, without limitation, freestanding columns and footings for all columns), provanded that such use shall not encroach on the interior of the Premises unless (i) all work carried on by Landlord with respect to such encroachment shall be done during hours when the Premises are not open for business and otherwise shall be carried out in such a manner as not to unreasonably interfere with Tenant's operations in the Premises, (ii) Landlord, at its expense, shall provande any security services to the Premises required by such work, and (iii) Landlord, at its expense, shall repair all damage to the Premises resulting from such work.

ARTICLE X
COMMON AREAS

Section 10.1. Use of Common Areas.

Landlord grants to Tenant and its agents, employees and customers a non-exclusive license to use the Common Areas in common with others during the Term, subject to the exclusive control and management thereof at all times by Landlord or others and subject, further, to the rights of Landlord set forth in Sections 9.5 and 10.2.

Section 10.2. Management and Operation of Common Areas.

Landlord will operate and maintain, or will cause to be operated and maintained, the Common Areas in a manner deemed by Landlord to be reasonable and appropriate and in the best interests of the Shopping Center. Landlord will have the right (i) to establish, modify and enforce reasonable rules and regulations with respect to the Common Areas; (ii) to enter into, modify and terminate easement and other agreements pertaining to the use and maintenance of the Common Areas; (iii) to enforce parking charges (by operation of meters or otherwise) with appropriate provisions for free parking ticket valandation by tenants; (iv) to close all or any portion of the Common Areas to such extent as may, in the opinion of Landlord, be necessary to prevent a dedication thereof or the accrual of any rights to any person or to the public therein; (v) to close temporarily any or all portions of the Common Areas; (vi) to discourage non customer parking; and (vii) to do and perform such other acts in and to saand areas and improvements as in the exercise of good business judgment, Landlord shall determine to be andvisable.

Section 10.3. Employee Parking Areas.

Tenant and its employees shall park their cars only in such areas designated for that purpose by Landlord. Upon request by Landlord, Tenant shall furnish Landlord with State automobile license numbers assigned to Tenant's car or cars and cars used by its employees and shall thereafter notify Landlord of any changes in such information within five (5) days after such changes occur. If Tenant or its employees shall fail to park their cars in the designated parking areas, then, without limiting any other remedy which Landlord may pursue in the event of Tenant's default, Landlord, after giving notice to Tenant, shall have the right to charge Tenant, as Andditional Rental, the sum of Ten Dollars ($10.00) per day per car parked in violation of the provisions of this Section. Tenant shall notify its employees in writing of the provisions of this Section.

Section 10.4. Tenant to Share Expense of Common Areas.

Tenant will pay Landlord, as Andditional Rental, a proportionate share of Landlord's Operating Costs which shall be computed by multiplying Landlord's Operating Costs (less any contribution to such costs and expenses mande by the owner or operator of any Anchor Store in the Shopping Center) by a fraction, the numerator of which is Tenant's Floor Area and the denominator of which is Landlord's Leased Floor Area. Such proportionate share shall be paand by Tenant in monthly installments in such amounts as are estimated and billed by Landlord at the beginning of each twelve (12) month period commencing and ending on dates designated by Landlord, each installment being due on the first day of each calendar month. At any time during any such twelve (12) month period, Landlord may reestimate Tenant's proportionate share of Landlord's Operating Costs and thereafter andjust Tenant's monthly installments payable during such twelve (12) month period to reflect more accurately Tenant's proportionate share of Landlord's Operating Costs. Within one hundred twenty (120) days (or such andditional time thereafter as is reasonable under the circumstances) after the end of each such twelve (12) month period, Landlord shall deliver to Tenant a statement of Landlord's Operating Costs for such twelve (12) month period and the monthly installments paand or payable shall be andjusted between Landlord and Tenant, and Tenant shall pay Landlord or Landlord shall credit Tenant's account (or, if such andjustment is at the end of the Term, Landlord shall pay Tenant), as the case may be, within fifteen (15) days of receipt of such statement, such amounts as may be necessary to effect such andjustment. Upon reasonable notice, Landlord shall make available for Tenant's inspection (which inspection shall be at Tenant's sole cost and expense) at Landlord's office, during normal business hours, Landlord's records relating to Landlord's Operating Costs for such preceding twelve (12) month period. Failure of Landlord to provande the statement called for hereunder within the time prescribed shall not relieve Tenant from its obligations hereunder.

Section 10.5. "Landlord's Operating Costs" Defined.

The term "Landlord's Operating Costs" means all costs and expenses incurred by or on behalf of Landlord in operating, managing, insuring, securing and maintaining the Common Areas pursuant to Section 10.2. "Landlord's Operating Costs" includes, but is not limited to, all costs and expenses of operating, maintaining, repairing, lighting, signing, cleaning, painting, striping, policing and security of the Common Areas (including the cost of uniforms, equipment and employment taxes); alarm and life safety systems; insurance, including, without limitation, liability insurance for personal injury, death and property damage, all-risks casualty insurance (including coverage against fire, flood, theft or other casualties), worker's compensation insurance or similar insurance covering personnel, fandelity bonds for personnel, insurance against liability for assault and battery, defamation and claims of false arrest occurring on and about the Common Areas, plate glass insurance for glass exclusively serving the Common Areas; the costs and expenses of maintenance of all exterior glass; maintenance of sprinkler systems; removal of water, snow, ice, trash and debris; regulation of traffic; surcharges levied upon or assessed against parking spaces or areas by governmental or quasi-governmental authorities, payments toward mass transit or car pooling facilities or otherwise as required by governmental or quasi-governmental authorities; costs and expenses in connection with maintaining federal, state or local governmental ambient air and environmental standards; the cost of all materials, supplies and services purchased or hired therefor; operation of public toilets; installing and renting of signs; fire protection; maintenance, repair and replacement of utility systems serving the Common Areas, including, but not limited to, water, sanitary sewer and storm water lines and other utility lines, pip and conduits; costs and expenses of maintaining and operating sewage treatment facilities, if any; costs and expenses of inspecting and depreciation of machinery and equipment used in the operation and maintenance of the Common Areas and personal property taxes and other charges (including, but not limited to, financing, leasing or rental costs) incurred in connection with such equipment; costs and expenses of the coordination and use of truck docks and loading facilities; costs and expenses of repair or replacement of awnings, paving, curbs, walkways, landscaping, drainage, pipes, ducts, conduits and similar items, plate glass, lighting facilities, floor coverings, and the roof; costs and expenses of planting, replanting, replacing and displaying flowers, shrubbery and planters; costs and expenses incurred in the purchase or rental of music program services and loudspeaker systems, including furnishing electricity therefor; costs of provanding light and power to the Common Areas; costs of provanding energy to beat, ventilate and air-condition the Common Areas and the operation, maintenance, and repair of equipment required therefor (including, without limitation, the costs of energy management systems serving the Shopping Center Area); cost of water services, if any, furnished by Landlord for the non-exclusive use of all tenants; parcel pick-up and delivery services; and andministrative costs attributable to the Common Areas for onsite personnel and an overheand cost equal to fifteen percent (15%) of the total costs and expenses of operating and maintaining the Common Areas. Landlord may elect to amortize any of the foregoing costs and expenses over a useful life determined in accordance with generally accepted accounting principles.

Section 10.6. Mall Heating, Ventilating and Air-Conditioning Equipment Contribution Rate.

In each Rental Year, Tenant shall pay Landlord annually (in twelve (12) equal monthly installments together with the Annual Basic Rental), as Andditional Rental, an amount (the "Mall Heating, Ventilating and Air Conditioning Equipment Contribution") determined by multiplying the Mall Heating, Ventilating and Air-Conditioning Equipment Contribution Rate by Tenant's Floor Area.

Appendix 3:

Purchase and Sale Agreement

Seller's Form of Purchase and Sale Agreement

Parties

Agreement made this _____ day of _____, _____ between _____ hereinafter called the Seller, and _____ hereinafter called the Buyer.

Description

The Seller agrees to sell and the Buyer agrees to buy the following described premises:

Fixtures and Improvements

Said premises shall include all buildings and improvements located thereon and all fixtures belonging to the Seller used in connection therewith including the following:

Quality of Title

Said premises are to be conveyed by a good and sufficient _____ deed of the Seller conveying a good and clear record and marketable title to the same, free from all encumbrances, except:

(a) provisions of building and zoning laws and regulations;
(b) party wall agreements;
(c) taxes assessed for the current year not due and payable at the time of closing;
(d) water and sewerage, and municipal betterment charges and assignments;
(e) easements and restrictions of record so far as the same are in force and applicable;
(f) _____.

All instruments and plans delivered to the buyer to effect the conveyance shall be in a form sufficient to entitle them to be recorded under applicable laws and regulations.

Registered Land

If the title to the premises is registered, the seller shall deliver to the buyer a deed and any other documents in a form sufficient to entitle the buyer to obtain a Certificate of Title to the premises.

Time for Performance

The deed shall be delivered and the purchase price paid at _____ on the _____ day of _____, _____ at _____ unless otherwise agreed. It is agreed that time is of the essence of this agreement.

Payment of Purchase Price

Buyer is to pay as the purchase price the sum of $_____ of which $_____ have been paid this day and the remainder of $_____ are to be paid in cash or certified or cashier's checks at the time of delivery of the deed.

Possession and Condition of Premises

Full possession of the premises free of tenants or occupants, except as herein provided, is to be delivered to the buyer at the time of delivery of the deed. The premises are to be delivered in the same condition as they are now reasonable use and wear of the buildings thereon, and damage by fire or other casualty excepted.

Insurance

The buildings on said premises shall, until the full performance of this agreement, be kept insured by the seller against fire or other casualty loss in the amount of $_____ .

Adjustments

Water and sewer use charges, rents, premiums on insurance policies, fuel located in tanks on the premises, and taxes for the current year shall be apportioned and adjusted as of the day of delivery of the deed.

If the amount of said taxes is not known as of the time of delivery of the deed they shall be apportioned on the basis of the taxes assessed for the preceeding year with a reapportionment as soon as the new tax rate and valuation can be ascertained.

If the taxes apportioned pursuant to this paragraph are subsequently reduced by abatement, the amount of such abatement, less the reasonable cost of obtaining the same, shall be apportioned between the buyer and seller.

Inability of Seller to Perform

If the seller shall be unable to give proper title to the premises as provided herein, or if the premises at the time set for conveyance shall not be in the condition required by this agreement, then the seller shall be given thirty (30) days in which to remove any defect in title or to restore the premises to proper condition.

In the event that the seller fails to remove such defect or to restore the premises within such time, any payment made under this agreement shall be refunded and all obligations of the parties shall cease and this agreement shall be void without recourse to either party.

Option of Buyer to Accept Defective Title or Premises

Where title is defective the buyer may, at either the original time for performance or at any extended time for performance, at (his) (her) option, accept such title as the seller can then deliver, paying the full contract price therefor.

The buyer may also at (his) (her) option accept premises which have been damaged by fire or other casualty, paying the full contract price therefor and receiving from the seller a conveyance of title along with an assignment of the rights to any insurance proceeds collectible as a result of such fire or casualty.

Merger by Acceptance

The acceptance of a deed by the buyer or (his) (her) nominee shall be deemed to be full performance of this agreement, except with respect to those obligations which are by the terms of this agreement to survive the delivery of the deed, or are to be performed after the delivery of the deed.

Use of Purchase Money to Clear Title

The seller may at the time of delivery of the deed apply any part or all of the purchase price for the purpose of discharging any encumbrances then on the premises.

Broker's Commission

A broker's fee of $_____ will be paid by the seller to _____ if and when the purchase price is paid in full to the seller and a deed is accepted by the buyer, and not otherwise.

Deposits

All deposits shall be held by _____ in accordance with the terms of this agreement, and shall be accounted for at the closing.

Default by Buyer—Effect

If the buyer fails to perform as required by this agreement then all deposits made hereunder may, at the option of the seller, be retained as liquidated damages.

Recording or Assignment of Contract

If the buyer shall record this agreement in the registry of deeds or assign his rights under the agreement to another, then, at the option of the seller, the buyer shall be deemed to be in default under the agreement and the seller's obligations under the agreement shall be at an end.

Financing Contingency

The buyer agrees to apply forthwith for a mortgage loan from a bank or other institutional lender. The mortgage loan applied for shall be for not more than _____ for not less than _____ years at a rate of interest not to exceed _____ percent per annum.

If the buyer, having applied for such a loan to at least three such lenders, and otherwise having used due diligence, shall be unable to obtain a commitment for a loan within _____ days, then this agreement shall be null and void and all deposits made by the buyer shall be returned to (him) (her) forthwith.

If the buyer does not notify the seller within _____ days that (he) (she) has been unable to obtain a loan commitment, then the buyer shall be deemed to have waived the provisions of this paragraph and the agreement shall be unconditionally binding.

Broker as Party

The undersigned broker(s) joins as a party in this agreement insofar as its provisions apply to (him)(her)(it)(them).

Construction of Agreement

This is a Massachusetts contract. It sets forth the entire agreement between the parties. The buyer acknowledges that (he)(she) has inspected the premises which are the subject of this agreement and that the seller has made no warranties or representations respecting the premises other than as set forth in this agreement.

Additional Provisions

_____   _____

Buyer   Seller

_____   _____

Buyer   Seller

               _____

             Broker

Seller's Form of Inspection Contingency Clause

For a period of _____ days after the date on which this agreement is signed, the buyer shall have the right at (his) (her) own expense to have the premises inspected to ascertain:

1) That the premises, including all fixtures and mechanical systems are structurally and mechanically sound;
2) that the premises are free of wood destroying pests of any kind;
3) that the premises are free from lead based paint or other material which would be a violation of G.L. c. 111.

If the buyer does not notify the seller within _____ days that (he) (she) has received an unsatisfactory inspection report respecting the premises, then the buyer shall be deemed to have waived the provisions of this paragraph and the agreement shall be unconditionally binding, except as otherwise provided.

Appendix 4:

Exclusive Authorization

and Right to Sell

FORM 1

EXCLUSIVE AUTHORIZATION AND RIGHT TO SELL

Realtors In consideration of the services of Jon Douglas Company (Broker), the undersigned (Seller) hereby employs Broker exclusively and irrevocably for a period of 180 days beginning _____, 19___ to sell the property situated in _____, County of _____, State of California, described as

JON DOUGLAS COMPANY follows: _____ (Property). Check box(es) for appropriate attached addenda which are made a part hereof by reference: ☐ Condominium ☐ Other

Included in the purchase price shall be all oil and mineral rights and leases held by Seller, if any, all tacked down carpets, drapes, window treatments, attached fixtures and all built-ins, TV antennas, garage door openers, pool and spa equipment, security system (if owned by Seller), all existing landscaping including trees and shrubs, items permanently attached to the Property and:_____

Excluded from the purchase price: _____

Seller hereby grants Broker the exclusive and irrevocable right to sell the Property within said time for _____ Dollars ($_____) all cash or terms of _____ or other terms to be agreed upon at the time of sale. Broker is authorized to accept deposits at time of sale.

NOTICE: THE AMOUNT OR RATE OF REAL ESTATE COMMISSIONS IS NOT FIXED BY LAW. THEY ARE SET BY EACH BROKER INDIVIDUALLY AND MAY BE NEGOTIABLE BETWEEN THE SELLER AND BROKER.

1. COMMISSIONS. Seller agrees to pay Broker as commission ____% of the selling price if the Property is sold[4] during the term hereof, or any

extension thereof, by Broker, or by Seller, or by another broker or through any other source. If the Property is withdrawn from sale, transferred or leased during the term hereof or any extension thereof, Seller agrees to pay Broker said percent of the above listed price. Seller agrees to execute an irrevocable assignment to Broker of a portion of Seller's sale proceeds in an amount equal to the commission set forth herein.

2. COMPENSATION. Seller agrees to pay Broker the compensation provided for above if the Property is sold, leased or transferred within 180 days after the termination of this authorization or any extension thereof to anyone with whom Broker or any subagents have negotiated, have shown the Property, or to any parties whom Broker or any subagents had informed of the Property during the term hereof or any extension thereof provided Broker has delivered to Seller, either personally or by mail, notice in writing, including the names of such parties within ten (10) days after termination of this authorization or any extension thereof except that Broker shall not be required to furnish Seller with the names of any parties who have submitted written offers to purchase the Property. Seller further agrees to register these names and the names of all parties who have submitted written offers to purchase the Property and exclude them from any exclusive agency and/or right to sell listing Seller may grant to any licensed real estate

broker within 180 days of the termination of this authorization or any extension thereof.

3. **ESCROW.** If an escrow is entered into by Seller and subsequently cancelled, this agreement shall terminate on the termination date hereof which may have been extended, or thirty (30) days from the date escrow is cancelled, whichever is later. Escrow is deemed cancelled when all parties thereto cancel same in writing and deliver said cancellation to escrow holder.

4. **SUBAGENTS.** Seller authorizes Broker to cooperate with any and all other licensed real estate brokers as subagents.

5. **TITLE.** Evidence of title shall be a California Land Title Association standard coverage policy of title insurance and shall be paid for by Seller. Jon Douglas Company, which may be serving as a broker in connection with this real estate transaction, has a financial interest in Equity Title Company and Camden Escrow Services, or is owned by someone who does.

6. **DEPOSITS.** If deposits or amounts paid on account of the purchase price are retained by Seller, Broker shall be entitled to one-half thereof but not to exceed the amount of the commission.

7. **PEST CONTROL INSPECTION.** Seller agrees to deliver to buyer as soon as possible prior to transfer of title a current termite inspection report and certification by a licensed pest control operator, pursuant to California Business and Professions Code, Section 8519, of all buildings on the Property. Seller shall pay through escrow the cost of all corrective work recommended in said report to repair damage caused by infestation or infection by wood-destroying pests or organisms, dry rot or fungi and all work to correct conditions that cause such infestation or infection including but not limited to water testing of all showers, any repairs required and replacement of any tile removed to make such repairs. Any preventive work to correct conditions usually deemed likely to lead to infestation or infection by wood-destroying pests or organisms, dry rot or fungi, but where no evidence of existing infestation or infection is found with respect to such

conditions, is not the responsibility of Seller and such work shall be done, if requested by buyer, at the expense of buyer. If inspection of inaccessible areas is recommended in the report, buyer shall be given the option of accepting and approving the report without inspection of such areas or requesting further inspection be made at buyer's expense. If further inspection is made and infestation, infection or damage is found, repair of such damage and all work to correct conditions that caused such infestation or infection shall be at the expense of Seller. If no infestation, infection or damage is found, any repair of entry and the cost of closure of the inaccessible areas shall be at the expense of buyer. Seller agrees, in accordance with Seller's legal obligation, to disclose all current pest control reports to buyer. Seller's obligation shall be limited to providing a certified completion notice; should buyer choose another, more expensive contractor, buyer shall be responsible for the cost in excess of the charges proposed by Seller's contractor or for a contractor who recommends more extensive work. Seller acknowledges that Broker is not responsible for inadequate inspection or repair by licensed pest control operators.

8.   RESIDENTIAL PROPERTY REPORT. If applicable, Seller shall obtain and deliver to buyer prior to close of escrow a copy of the Report of Residential Property Records and Pending Special Assessment Liens as required by Los Angeles Municipal Code, Sections 96.300-96.310 or Residential Building Record as required by Chapter 2, Article IX of the Santa Monica Municipal Code or any similar code requirements of other municipalities.

9.   SMOKE DETECTORS, IMPACT HAZARD GLAZING AND WATER CONSERVATION DEVICES. State and local ordinances may require the installation of smoke detector(s), impact hazard glazing and/or water conservation devices. If required, smoke detector(s), impact hazard glazing and/or water conservation devices shall be installed, inspected by the appropriate city or county agency, required compliance reports obtained and appropriate notification given to buyer and/or the Department of Building and Safety.

10.   ATTORNEYS' FEES. If any action be instituted regarding this agreement to enforce or interpret any of the terms and provisions contained herein, the prevailing parts, in such action shall be entitled to such reasonable attorneys' fees, costs and expenses as may be fixed by the court.

11.   ENTIRE AGREEMENT. There are no oral agreements or representations not contained herein.

12.   DUE DILIGENCE. In consideration of the execution of the foregoing, the undersigned Broker agrees to use diligence in procuring a buyer. Seller shall cooperate by making the Property available for showing at reasonable times and shall immediately refer to Broker all inquiries of any party interested in the Property. Seller shall take reasonable precautions to safeguard, protect and insure valuable personal property items that might be accessible during the showing of the Property. Said personal property shall include, but not be limited to, jewelry, artifacts, currency and securities.

13.   CONDITION OF PROPERTY, SYSTEMS AND APPLIANCES. Seller represents that there is not presently a Notice of Default recorded against the Property and that the Property is not an asset which is part of any current bankruptcy proceedings. Seller represents that the heating, wiring, plumbing, air conditioning, if any, and all other mechanical apparatus are presently in normal working order and Seller has no knowledge of any physical, geological, soil, drainage or structural defects affecting the land or the improvements of the Property except as follows:[1] _____.

To the best of Seller's knowledge, the Property conforms with all applicable ordinances, laws, zoning and governmental regulations.

14. **SIGN.** Seller authorizes Broker to place a "For Sale" sign on the Property.

15. **MULTIPLE LISTING SERVICE.** Seller authorizes Broker to submit all listing and sales information to any multiple listing service that Broker deems appropriate.

16. **AUTHORITY.** Seller warrants that Seller is the owner of the Property or has the authority to execute this agreement on behalf of the owner and acknowledges having received a copy of this agreement.

17. **FOREIGN INVESTMENT IN REAL PROPERTY TAX ACT.** Seller acknowledges that the Foreign Investment In Real Property Tax Act requires the buyer of the Property to withhold ten percent (10%) of the amount realized by Seller in the sale of the Property unless Seller, or this transaction, is able to qualify as an exclusion to the Act. Seller may so qualify by signing a certification stating that Seller is not a "foreign person" as defined by the Act or by buyer signing a certification stating that the amount realized by the sale does not exceed $300,000 and buyer intends to use the Property as a residence. Seller may also gain an exemption by furnishing buyer with a "qualifying statement" approved by the Internal Revenue Service. If Seller has any questions regarding the application of the Act, or Seller's obligations thereunder, Seller agrees to contact Seller's legal counsel. Seller recognizes that Seller may be required to furnish buyer, prior to close of escrow, with a Non-Foreign Affidavit (IRC Section 1445) in order to exempt buyer from buyer's withholding requirements.

18. **REAL ESTATE TRANSFER DISCLOSURE STATEMENT.** If the Property consists of at least one (1) but not more than four (4) residential units, Seller shall complete and deliver to buyer a Real Estate Transfer Disclosure Statement as provided in California Civil Code, Section 1102 et seq.

19. Seller's Initials

    _____/_____ **RENT CONTROL.** By initialing this paragraph, Seller acknowledges that the Property may be subject to a rent control law. Seller hereby acknowledges that Seller has been advised to check with legal

counsel and/or the rent control board to determine Seller's rights and obligations under the law and further represents that the Property is not presently leased for any rental in excess of the maximum allowable rental permitted under such rent control law and that any present rentals are in full compliance with such law. Seller further acknowledges that Seller is not relying upon any advice from Broker regarding said rent control law.

SELLER:_____   ADDRESS:_____
SELLER:_____   _____

JON DOUGLAS COMPANY (BROKER)   TELEPHONE:_____

ACCEPTED BY:_____

Appendix 5:
Residential Contracting Agreement

RESIDENTIAL CONTRACTING AGREEMENT

This agreement is made on
between

(hereinafter called "Contractor')

(hereinafter called "Owner"
for the renovation of   (hereinafter called
the "Project").

1. The Contract Documents;
The contract documents are:
this Agreement signed by the Contractor and Owner;
attached document titled Specifications and Terms for the renovation of
Street (hereinafter called "Specifications and Terms");
Drawings A01, A02, A03, A04, A08, A10-1, A10-2, A10-3, A11, A12, A13, and A14
signed by

2. Description of the Project:
The project consists of fully completing in   all the work described in
the attached Specifications and Terms and in the attached drawings.

3. The Contract Price:
The contract price for completing all the work on the project shall be $210,165.

4. Payments:
Payments shall be made as follows:
$ 21,000 upon signing of the contract;
$ 42,000 upon completion of all demolition and framing work;

$ 42,000 upon completion of all rough plumbing work, rough electrical work , and rough mechanical work (including heating and air conditioning);

$ 31,500 upon completion of all Blue Board and plaster work and all installation of windows work;

$ 31,500 upon completion of all finish carpentry work (including installation of all cabinets and countertops);

$ 42,165 upon final completion of the work on the project and verification by the Owner and Contractor of the work as having been satisfactorily complete, which verification shall take place promptly after completion.

5. Allowances:

The contract price includes the following allowances:

(i)   allowance of $500 for the purchase of the door hardware indicated in subsections 3 and 4 of the doors, frames and hardware section (#08200) of the attached Specifications and Terms:

(ii) allowance of $500 for the purchase of bathroom accessories indicated in the bathroom accessories sections (#10800) of the attached Specifications and Terms;

(iii) allowance of $11,750 for the purchase of cabinets indicated in subsection 1,2, and 3 of the pre-fabricated cabinets section (#12375) of the attached Specifications and Terms;

(iv) allowance of $5,850 for the purchase of countertops indicated in subsections 4,5, and 6 of the tile and stone section (#09300 and #09600) of the attached Specifications and Terms;

(v)   allowance of $4,000 for the purchase of plumbing fixtures and fittings indicated in subsections 7 and 8 of the plumbing fixtures section (#15440) of the attached Specifications and Terms:

(vi) allowance of $2,500 for the purchase of electrical fixtures and electrical devices indicated in subsections 10 and 11 of the Electrical section (#16000) of the attached Specifications and Terms;

These allowances shall be used only for the purchase of the materials and equipment indicated in (i)-(vi) above. The purchase of all other materials and equipment is already included in the contract price.

All allowances shall be calculated at the contractor's net prices (after including all applicable trade discounts) including taxes plus a markup of 10% , and the contractor shall provide the Owner with a copy of suppliers' invoices and receipts. The allowances shall be solely for the purchase of materials or equipment; the costs of installation, handling at the site, overhead and profits are all already included in the contract price. Any difference between the allowance and the Contractor's said net prices (plus the 10% markup) shall be either added to the contract price or deleted from it as the case may be, and the final payment will be adjusted up or down to reflect such changes, if any, in the contract price. Prior to purchasing any materials or equipment using the allowance, the Contractor shall notify the Owner of their prices, and the Owner shall then have the right to have other materials or equipment used or to supply the materials or equipment by himself; any part of the allowance not used because of the Owner's decision to supply the materials or equipment by himself will be deleted from the contract price.

6. Completion of Work:

The Contractor shall complete all the work on the project within fourteen weeks after receiving the permit required to begin the work on the Project.

If the work is not completed by the Contractor by   the liquidated damages to the Owner shall be $140 for each day of extra delay and the final payment will be reduced accordingly.

7. Insurance:

The Contractor shall be responsible to the Owner or any third party for any property damage or bodily injury caused by himself, his employees or his subcontractors in the performance of, or as a result of, the work under this agreement. The Contractor shall carry insurance to cover such damage or injury and shall provide the Owner with a copy of his certificate of insurance.

8. Subcontracting:

The Contractor agrees that, notwithstanding any agreement for materials and/or labor between Contractor and a third party, Contractor shall be responsible to Owner for completion of all work on the project.

9. Permits:

The Contractor shall apply for and obtain all construction-related permits.

10. The Architect:

The architect for the project shall be

, or, if she is replaced by the Owner, the architect that shall be then selected by the Owner.

11. Modification:

This agreement, including the provisions relating to price and payment schedule cannot be changed except by a written agreement signed by both Contractor and Owner.

12. Other Terms and conditions:

All the terms, conditions, and requirements that appear in the attached Specifications and Terms are part of this agreement and are hereby incorporated in it.

Specifications and Terms for the
Renovation of

01000 GENERAL REQUIREMENTS

1. The Contractor shall be assumed to have visited the site and to have familiarized himself with all pre-existing conditions.
2. All work shall be performed in strict compliance with the provisions of the local Building Code and all other applicable governmental codes and regulations.
3. All work shall be carried out in compliance with the requirements of the Owner prior to commencement of the work. The Contractor shall submit all necessary construction permits and certificates of insurance to the Owner.
4. All work shall be executed in a workmanlike manner and in conformance with manufacturers specifications, by mechanics skilled in the work and familiar with the materials to be installed. The Contractor shall submit samples and/or manufacture's data of any items requested by Owner or Architect.
5. The use of the word "Provide" or "Provided" in connection with an item specified is intended to mean, unless otherwise noted, that such item shall be furnished and installed by the Contractor with all required accessories and connected as required.
6. The Contractor shall coordinate all cutting, fitting, and patching of work that may be required to make all parts come together properly and fit to receive or be received by work of other contractors shown upon or reasonably implied by the drawings and notes.
7. The Contractor shall verify all dimensions at the site. The Contractor shall not scale the drawings nor rely on the written dimensions indicated on them. The Contractor shall notify the Architect of any discrepancies between the drawings, these specifications and field conditions and request clarification prior to commencing work affected.
8. The construction area shall be maintained by the Contractor in a clean and orderly condition and all trash and debris shall be promptly removed from the building.
9. At completion of work, the Contractor shall remove waste materials, rubbish, tools, equipment, machinery and surplus materials, and clean all exposed surfaces. The Contractor shall leave Project clean and ready for occupancy.
10. In all matters not specified in the Contract or the Specifications, the provisions of AIA Document A201, General Conditions of the Contract for Construction, shall govern and should be regarded as being part of the Contract.
11. The Contractor shall warrant that, for one year after substantial completion, all movable parts shall remain in good operating condition; roofs, floors, walls, windows, drains, valves, etc. shall remain watertight and in good working condition; all systems in the building shall remain in good operating condition; and all work performed by

or through Contractor shall be free from defects of materials and/or workmanship. The Contractor agrees that he will repair and replace all such defective work during the terms of this warranty at his own expense.

12. Before final payment, the Contractor shall file with Owner a release or waiver of liens; a complete set of manuals containing manufacturers' instructions for maintenance and operation of each piece of equipment; and a Certificate of Occupancy.

13. Contractor shall carry "all risk" insurance to cover the costs of this work. Contractor shall present certificate of insurance at the time the contract is signed.

14. All substitutions must be approved by the Owner in writing. Approval of the substitutions shall not relieve the Contractor from responsibility for complying with the drawings and specifications, and the Contractor shall be responsible for any related changes resulting from substitutions. All substitutions shall be transmitted as a Change Order for review by the Owner. All such Change Orders shall record whether the substitution is a credit or an addition to the Contract.

15. All change orders must be approved in writing by the Owner or Architect. Any work performed prior to written approval shall be considered within the contract price.

16. Contractor shall coordinate the work with the Department of Public Works Water Department regarding the work to, or replacement of, the main water line from the street. Contractor shall restore sidewalk, curb, and lawn as required.

17. 6 December 1998 document and SK-1, SK-1a and SK-2 dated 9 December 1998 from the structural engineer,   is a part of the scope of work, Re: Outline specifications for Basement Floor Slab, Foundation Walls, Masonry for First Floor Fireplace/Boiler flue, and Floor Leveling.

02070 SELECTIVE DEMOLITION

1. Demolition shall be included as a part of this contract. Scope of demolition work shall include the removal of all existing construction required to accommodate new work shown. Scope of demolition work shall include all interior partitions, ceilings, Basement partitions and wood floor, the front chimney and fireplace from the First Floor through and including to the Roof, and the rear chimney from the Basement through and including to the Roof. The Contractor shall remove abandoned utilities and systems.
2. Demolished materials shall be removed from site. Debris shall not accumulate on site.
3. All items removed during demolition that are scheduled to be reinstalled shall be temporarily stored in a protected area to prevent damage. Prior to reinstallation, these items shall be cleaned and restored to the highest quality possible. The Contractor shall protect all materials and components that are indicated to remain during the course of the construction.
4. Contractor shall save and store, at Owner's designated area, all trims and doors that will not be used in the renovation.
5. At Owner's request, Contractor shall demolish and remove from the site existing garden shed and concrete platform.
6. Contractor shall remove the exterior fire escape and ladder and shall patch at demolished areas.

02200 EARTHWORK

1. The Contractor shall provide suitable fill from offsite if on-site quantities are insufficient or unacceptable and shall legally dispose of excess fill offsite.

03550 CONCRETE FLOOR TOPPING

1. The Contractor shall provide 3500 psi concrete floor topping over existing concrete slab to repair and level floors at the Basement in accordance with structural engineer's document attached.

04200 UNIT MASONRY

1. The Contractor shall repair at Basement foundation wall, per structural engineer's document attached.

06100 ROUGH CARPENTRY

1. The Contractor shall provide rough carpentry work:

    a. Wood framing.
    b. Sheathing.
    c. Underlayments.
    d. Backing panels for utilities.
    e. Nailer, blocking, furring and sleepers.
2. The Contractor shall comply with governing codes and regulations. The Contractor shall deliver, handle, and store materials in accordance with manufacturer's instructions.
3. The Contractor shall provide blocking for all mounted items including:
    a. Casework and shelving.
    b. Handrails and railings.
    c. Toilet accessories.
4. The Contractor shall comply with recommendations of NFPA Manual for House Framing, NFPA Recommended Nailing Schedule, and NFPA National Design Specifications for Wood Construction.
5. The Contractor shall follow and implement structural engineer's documents for (i) beam and column specification and installation procedure and for (ii) floor leveling.
6. Existing stair from First Floor to Basement shall be shored and framed to make sound.
7. The Contractor shall survey existing roof and repair all areas that have failed.

06200 FINISH CARPENTRY

1. Unless otherwise noted, all millwork shall be fabricated with Custom Grade standards of the Architectural Woodwork Institute. Natural finish and plastic laminate surfaced millwork shall be of Custom Grade; painted finish millwork shall be of Custom Grade.
2. Interior trim shall be sizes and shapes to match existing profile. All existing interior trim and casings shall be saved and reinstalled.
3. Exterior painted wood trim, soffits shall be #1, flat sawn, non finger-jointed clear Common Pine, sizes to match that of existing.
4. Existing framing of deck shall be removed and new deck framing shall be pressured treated Pine. Exterior roof decking shall be 1 x 4 vertical grain fir.
5. The Contractor shall provide and install new wood treads at Rear Stair and Attic Stair to match existing at front stair, clear finish.
6. Thresholds between dissimilar floor surfaces shall be clear finish wood.
7. Closet shelving shall be ¾" Melamine, color white, adjustable on white brackets and standards.
9. Closet bars shall be chrome finish and shall be at locations and heights chosen by the Owner.

07110 SHEET MEMBRANE WATERPROOFING

1. The Contractor shall provide EPDM, Sure-Seal by Carlisle or equal, gauge 1 and 1/16 inch, at Second Floor roof underneath exterior deck.

07120 FLUID-APPLIED WATERPROOFING

1. The Contractor shall provide foundation waterproofing per structural engineer's specifications.

07145 CEMENTITIOUS WATERPROOFING

1. The Contractor shall provide cementitious waterproofing on interior surfaces of foundation walls per structural engineer's specifications.

07200 INSULATION AND VAPOR BARRIERS

1. All interior face of exterior walls shall be gutted. The Contractor shall install continuous insulation and vapor barrier assembly.
2. Insulation:
   a. The Contractor shall provide unfaced fiberglass batt (min. R19) friction fit into stud cavities at all new exterior stud walls.
   b. The Contractor shall provide fiberglass batt (min. R33) between roof joists and rafters at ceilings and sloped roof areas.
3. Vapor barrier:
   The Contractor shall provide 6 mil. clear polyethylene vapor barrier for newly exposed cathedral ceiling.
4. The Contractor shall provide "Propervent" or similar vent chutes as necessary to provide air flow at attic and roof spaces.

07270 FIRESTOPPING

1. The Contractor shall provide firestopping insulation and caulking to prevent passage of flame and products of combustion through concealed spaces, openings between and around floors, and in fire-rated assemblies.

07310 SHINGLES

1. The Contractor shall provide sheathing, and shingles at roof patch areas.

07460 SIDING

1. The Contractor shall provide exterior siding to match existing at renovated areas.

07600 FLASHING AND SHEET METAL

1. The Contractor shall provide flashing around new windows.
2. The Contractor shall provide a continuous ridge vent and soffit vents.
3. The Contractor shall repair and/or replace gutters and downspouts. Existing drywells shall be abandoned and downspouts provided. All downspouts shall be diverted away from the building foundation.

07900 SEALANTS

1. The Contractor shall provide all sealers needed to create a completely watertight and weather tight building. The Contractor shall provide sealants between all interior and exterior dissimilar materials. The Contractor shall provide acrylic latex for typical exterior building joints. The Contractor shall provide mildew resistant silicone sanitary sealant for plumbing fixtures, countertops and ceramic tile joints. The Contractor shall provide acrylic latex sealant for interior joints at door frames, windows and elsewhere.

08200 DOORS, FRAMES AND HARDWARE

1. All existing doors shall be repaired, painted and reused. Existing passage sets and locksets shall be removed, and doors shall be prepared to receive new hardware sets.
2. Existing glazed door between the Dining Room and the Kitchen shall be saved and re-installed at the new opening to the Kitchen.
3. The Contractor shall provide new passage sets at all interior and exterior doors: Schlage Plymouth F Series #F10N626, with B160N626 at entry doors. The Contractor shall provide privacy set at all Bathroom doors: Schlage Plymouth F Series #F40N626.
4. The Contractor shall provide #B160N626 lockset at door from Guest Room to Corridor and from corridor to Dining Room.
5. The Contractor shall provide aluminum combination storm doors at all exterior doors.

08610 WOOD WINDOWS

1. All existing windows that are scheduled to remain shall receive new Harvey wood interior, vynil exterior, with Argon insulated glass, 1/1 sashes.
2. The Contractor shall provide and install new wood interior/clad exterior Andersen windows at Bathrooms, #F8, #F9 and #S10, (1) at Study #A3, and (2) at Study #A2.

3. The Contractor shall provide and install combination storm/screen windows at new work and at any existing windows that are missing the assembly. New units shall match existing ones.
4. The Contractor shall verify all dimensions before ordering.

08810 GLASS and GLAZING

1. The Contractor shall provide and install glass and glazing for all applications scheduled:
   a. Shower Door, Bathroom #S8: Century #CT-5, 3/8" tempered clear glass, white frame and (2) white towel/pull bars.
   b. Mirror: ¼" safety glass. Install with adhesives – no surface mounted slips.
   c. Re-glaze existing front door and glaze new window sash at#S8 and #F8 with ¼" architectural laminated glass with white interlayer.

09215 VENEER PLASTER

1. The Contractor shall provide veneer plaster over gypsum board for walls and ceilings, ASTM C 587 Imperial Finish, U.S. Gypsum or approved equal.

09250 DRYWALL

1. Wallboard shall be ½" thickness with tapered edge, specifically engineered to accept a skim coat plaster veneer.
2. The Contractor shall provide ½" thick cementitious backerboard ("Durock" or approved equivalent) for all walls and floors to receive ceramic tile finish. The Contractor shall provide 4 mil. Polyethylene film behind or beneath cementitious backerboard.
3. Fasteners shall be ASTM C 514 and ASTM C 646, Type S bugle head screws.
4. Galvanized steel corner beads, casing beads and control joints: U.S. Gypsum 800 series as applicable.

09300 TILE and 09600 STONE

1. New Bathrooms, Rm. No. F8, F9, S8, S10, A4 : The Contractor shall provide and install tiles:
   a. Floor: Refin 12" x 12", color Gonzago
   b. Walls: Bisquit, 6"x 6"
2. New Kitchen, Rm. No. F5: The Contractor shall provide and install tiles:
   a. Floor: Tivoli 13" x 13"
   b. Walls: Tivoli, 6.5" x 6.5"

3. The Contractor shall install tile following the manufacturers recommendations for surface prepared to provide a smooth and suitable uniform surface. Thinset with waterproof organic adhesive. The Contractor shall provide latex portland cement grout, color selected by Owner.
4. Kitchen, Rm. No. F5: The Contractor shall provide and install stone countertops as selected by Owner.
5. The Contractor shall provide and install Corian countertop with sink for Bathrooms S10 and A4: 100 Series, Glacier White.
6. The Contractor shall provide and install at the Master Bathroom stone countertops as selected by Owner.
7. The Contractor shall verify all dimensions and conditions before ordering.

09550 WOOD FLOORING

1. All wood floors shall be filled and patched with matching flooring, and finished per specifications.
2. Attic Rm. A2, and A3: The Contractor shall install matching wood floor at damaged areas as required and finish per specifications.
3. Foyer outside Attic Rms A2 and A3 shall receive new wood flooring to match A2 and A3 and shall be finished per specifications.

09900 PAINTING & FINISHING

1. All new exterior trim shall be primed per requirements of this section.
2. All wood floors shall be finished per the requirements of this section. Dry sweep and dust all surfaces before applying any finish.
3. All materials that are to receive painter's finish shall be filled, sanded and otherwise prepared for priming and finishing in accordance with the best practices of the trade. All nail holes, cracks, etc. shall be filled with a recommended type filler. Filler shall be applied after priming coats are dry on surfaces scheduled for priming. All knots, pitch pockets and sap streaks shall be shellacked before paint is applied.
4. Exterior wood trim: 1 coat primer, two coats oil based gloss paint.
   Exterior shingles: Power wash to remove all mildew and discoloration; one coat kills tinted plus one coat heavy body stain same color (or, if requested by owner, a shade darker) as existing color.
   Exterior decking: 2 coats Cabot clear decking stain.
   Exterior wood rails: 1 coat primer, two coats oil based gloss paint.
   Interior walls: 1 coat primer, two coats eggshell latex paint.
   Interior ceilings: 1 coat primer, two coats flat latex ceiling white paint.
   Interior trim: 1 coat primer, two coats satin alkyd enamel paint.
   Wood flooring: 3 coats oil-based satin polyurethane.
5. Paint shall be by Benjamin Moore or architect approved equivalent, colors to be selected by Owner.

10800 BATHROOM ACCESSORIES

1. The Contractor shall provide and install at all Bathrooms:
   a. GUSA Ginger #2325 polished chrome toilet paper holder
   b. GUSA Ginger Series #494 polished chrome towel bars. Refer to plans and elevations for sizes
   c. The Contractor shall polish chrome shower pole and wall brackets at Bathrooms #F9 and #S10.

11450 RESIDENTIAL EQUIPMENT

1. The Contractor shall provide plumbing, electrical and venting hook-up for all Owner supplied, Contractor installed appliances:

   Refrigerator: Frigidare Gallery FRS24F 35.25" w 67" h, side by side w/ ice & water
   Range: Frigidare Gallery FES388WECA 30" (electric)
   Oven Range Microwave (with hood): Frigidare Gallery FMT148 SS 30" w by 17" h
   Disposal: ISE batch feed ¾ hp with 5 year warranty
   Dishwasher: Frigidare Gallery FDB989GFC
   Washer and Dryer: Maytag model 7806 white, 27.5" w 27.5" d

12375 PRE FABRICATED CABINETS

1. The Contractor shall provide and install pre manufactured cabinets for the Kitchen Rm. No. 6:
   Metropolitan LesCare, Westbury with flat drawer face. Upgrade to dove tail wood drawer, blind corner and light valance. Pull to be Amerock #P-55BL.
2. The Contractor shall provide and install pre manufactured cabinets at Bathroom Nos. S8, S10, and A4:
   Metropolitan Richmond, color white.
3. The Contractor shall provide and install at Bathrooms No. F8, F9, and S8 Bathroom vanity cabinets as selected by owner.
4. The Contractor shall verify all dimensions and conditions before ordering and shall be responsible for coordination with cabinet manufactures.

15440 PLUMBING FIXTURES

1. The Contractor shall provide plumbing systems including supply, waste and vent systems for Kitchens and Bathrooms. Copper piping to be Type L.
2. The Contractor shall modify and extend existing service to accommodate new work.

The Contractor shall remove existing systems and piping no longer required.

3. Plumbing fixtures shall be installed in Bathroom Nos. F8, F9, S8, S10, and A4.
4. The Contractor shall provide rough plumbing connections for Rms. Nos. F7 and S7.
5. The Contractor shall provide plumbing fixtures for Kitchen, including ice maker line at refrigerator.
6. All plumbing lines at the Basement shall be brought tight to the joists to allow for maximum head room.
7. Fixture schedule:
   a. Toilet: American Standard Savona #RF2095.012.020
   b. Pedestal sink, #F8, F9: American Standard Cadet #0014.000.020
   c. Bathtub at #S8: American Standard Princeton #2395.202 ICH.020
   d. Bathtub at #F9 and S10: American Standard #2390.202 ICH.020
   e. Undermount lavatory, #S8, S10 and A4: American Standard Ovalyn II #0496.011.020
   f. Kitchen sink: Elkay #NG-3322-2
8. Fitting Schedule:
   a. Bathroom sink fitting: American Standard Reliant #2385.000.002
   b. Kitchen sink fitting: American Standard Reliant #4400.631.002
   c. Bath/shower fitting, #F9, S8, S10: American Standard Reliant #1495.502.002
9. The Contractor shall provide new washer/dryer hook-up.
10. The Contractor shall retain existing washer/dryer hook-up and utility sink at Basement.
11. The Contractor shall provide and install (2) gas fired hot water heaters at 75 gal. each.

15500 HEATING, VENTILATING and AIR CONDITIONING

1. The Contractor shall provide forced air mechanical systems including:
   a. Heating system including boiler.
   b. Ventilating system including fans, sheet metal work, registers, grilles and diffusers.
   c. Panasonic #FV05VQ exhaust fan at all Bathrooms.
   d. Air conditioning system including chiller.
   e. Piping distribution system and insulation.
   f. Temperature controls for a five (5) zone system: (1) zone for the Basement, (1) zone for Rooms #F7 and F9 of the First Floor, (1) zone for the rest of the First Floor, (1) zone for the second floor, and (1) zone for the Attic.
   g. Testing, balancing and adjusting.
2. The Contractor shall coordinate with Owner's room uses to provide adequate system for all areas.
3. The Contractor shall coordinate location of mechanical systems to avoid interference with location of other systems or construction. The Contractor shall notify Owner of conflicts which cannot be resolved.
4. The Contractor shall comply with SMACNA Duct Manual and Sheet Metal Construction for Ventilating and Air Conditioning systems.

5. Grilles and registers shall be approved by Owner.

16000 ELECTRICAL

1. the Contractor shall provide electrical systems including:
   a. Power
   b. Lighting
   c. Cable TV system
   d. Telephone and data outlets
2. The contractor shall modify and extend existing service to accommodate new work.
3. The Contractor shall comply with governing codes and regulations.
4. Arrangement of systems indicated on the drawings is diagrammatic, and indicates the the minimum requirements for electrical work. Site conditions shall determine the actual arrangement of conduits, boxes, and similar items.
5. The Contractor shall comply with the National Electrical Code and applicable local regulations.
6. All devices shall be white.
7. Gang multiple switching locations. The Contractor shall mount multiple types of controls as close together as possible at the same height.
8. The Contractor shall confirm all electrical devices with Owner prior to installation of rough electrical work.
9. The Contractor shall coordinate with the Owner's security system contractor.
10. Fixture schedule:
    a. Recessed down lights at Living Room, Dining Room, Kitchen
       Halo #H1499T75-1421 with 75W12VMR16
    b. Continuous under cabinet lights at Kitchen
       Lightolier Illuminator starter and joiners
    c. Track lighting. Refer to drawings for track lengths and number of track heads.
       Lightolier Radius track, color white.
       Lightolier #9148WH live end connector
       Lightolier #9149WH mini coupler
       Lightolier #9060WH monopoint
       Lightolier #PAR38 ring shade #8202/8248WH track head with 150W lamp
    d. Surface mounted wall fixture
       Lightolier Luna #40620 with 75WA19
    e. Surface mounted ceiling fixture at Bathrooms
       Lightolier #6701-WH with A19 75W lamp
    f. Pendant light fixture at Kitchen
       Lightolier Astra #4542-WH with 150W lamp
    g. Medicine cabinet light fixture
       Lightolier #5412-WH with (2) TT comp fluor. 10W lamps
    h. Exterior light fixture
       Lightolier Lumilyte #6560WH, with 75WA19
11. Electrical device schedule: .

a. switch: Leviton Decora Plus, white
b. receptacles: Leviton Decora Plus, white
c. telephon receptacle: Leviton Decora Plus, white
d. CTV receptacle: Leviton Decora Plus, white
e. rheostats: Lutron Diva, white
        1. incandescent preset for incandescent down lights and wall light
        2. electronic low-voltage for track lights
        3. magnetic low-voltage for halogen down lights

Appendix 6:
AAA Commercial
Arbitration Rules

Commercial Arbitration Rules

R-1. Agreement of Parties
The parties shall be deemed to have made these rules a part of their arbitration agreement whenever they have provided for arbitration by the AAA under its Commercial Arbitration Rules or for arbitration by the AAA of a domestic commercial dispute without specifying particular rules. These rules and any amendment of them shall apply in the form in effect at the time the demand for arbitration or submission agreement is received by the AAA. The parties, by written agreement, may vary the procedures set forth in these rules.

A dispute arising out of an employment relationship will be administered under the AAA's National Rules for the Resolution of Employment Disputes, unless all parties agree otherwise after the commencement of AAA administration.

R-2. AAA and Delegation of Duties

When parties agree to arbitrate under these rules, or when they provide for arbitration by the AAA and an arbitration is initiated under these rules, they thereby authorize the AAA to administer the arbitration. The authority and duties of the AAA are prescribed in the agreement of the parties and in these rules, and may be carried out through such of the AAA's representatives as it may direct. The AAA may, in its discretion, assign the administration of an arbitration to any of its offices.

R-3. National Panel of Arbitrators

The AAA shall establish and maintain a National Panel of Commercial Arbitrators and shall appoint arbitrators as provided in these rules. The term "arbitrator" in these rules refers to the arbitration panel, whether composed of one or more arbitrators and whether the arbitrators are neutral or party-appointed.

R-4. Initiation under an Arbitration Provision in a Contract

    (a) Arbitration under an arbitration provision in a contract shall be initiated in the following manner:

> The initiating party (the claimant) shall, within the time period, if any, specified in the contract(s), give to the other party (the respondent) written notice of its intention to arbitrate (the demand), which demand shall contain a statement setting forth the nature of the dispute, the names and addresses of all other parties, the amount involved, if any, the remedy sought, and the hearing locale requested.

> The claimant shall file at any office of the AAA two copies of the demand and two copies of the arbitration provisions of the contract, together with the appropriate filing fee as provided in the schedule included with these rules.

> The AAA shall confirm notice of such filing to the parties.

    (b) A respondent may file an answering statement in duplicate with the AAA within fifteen days after confirmation of notice of filing of the demand is sent by the AAA. The respondent shall, at the time of any such filing, send a copy of the answering statement to the claimant. If a counterclaim is asserted, it shall contain a statement setting forth the nature of the counterclaim, the amount involved, if any, and the remedy sought. If a counterclaim is made, the party making the counterclaim shall forward to the AAA with the answering statement the appropriate fee provided in the schedule included with these rules.

(c) If no answering statement is filed within the stated time, respondent will be deemed to deny the claim. Failure to file an answering statement shall not operate to delay the arbitration.

(d) When filing any statement pursuant to this section, the parties are encouraged to provide descriptions of their claims in sufficient detail to make the circumstances of the dispute clear to the arbitrator.

R-5. Initiation under a Submission

Parties to any existing dispute may commence an arbitration under these rules by filing at any office of the AAA two copies of a written submission to arbitrate under these rules, signed by the parties. It shall contain a statement of the nature of the dispute, the names and addresses of all parties, any claims and counterclaims, the amount involved, if any, the remedy sought, and the hearing locale requested, together with the appropriate filing fee as provided in the schedule included with these rules. Unless the parties state otherwise in the submission, all claims and counterclaims will be deemed to be denied by the other party.

R-6. Changes of Claim

After filing of a claim, if either party desires to make any new or different claim or counterclaim, it shall be made in writing and filed with the AAA. The party asserting such a claim or counterclaim shall provide a copy to the other party, who shall have fifteen days from the date of such transmission within which to file an answering statement with the AAA. After the arbitrator is appointed, however, no new or different claim may be submitted except with the arbitrator's consent.

R-7. Applicable Procedures

Unless the parties or the AAA in its discretion determines otherwise, the Expedited Procedures shall be applied in any case where no disclosed claim or counterclaim exceeds $75,000, exclusive of interest and arbitration costs. Parties may also agree to use the Expedited Procedures in cases involving claims in excess of $75,000. The Expedited Procedures shall be applied as described in §§ E-1 through E-10 of these rules, in addition to any other portion of these rules that is not in conflict with the Expedited Procedures. All other cases shall be administered in accordance with §§ R-1 through R-56 of these rules.

R-8. Jurisdiction

(a) The arbitrator shall have the power to rule on his or her own jurisdiction, including any objections with respect to the existence, scope, or validity of the arbitration agreement.

(b) The arbitrator shall have the power to determine the existence or validity of a contract of which an arbitration clause forms a part. Such an arbitration clause shall be treated as an agreement independent of the other terms of the contract. A decision by the arbitrator that the contract is null and void shall not for that reason alone render invalid the arbitration clause.

(c) A party must object to the jurisdiction of the arbitrator or to the arbitrability of a claim or counterclaim no later than the filing of the answering statement to the claim or counterclaim that gives rise to the objection. The arbitrator may rule on such objections as a preliminary matter or as part of the final award.

R-9.   Mediation

At any stage of the proceedings, the parties may agree to conduct a mediation conference under the Commercial Mediation Rules in order to facilitate settlement. The mediator shall not be an arbitrator appointed to the case. Where the parties to a pending arbitration agree to mediate under the AAA's rules, no additional administrative fee is required to initiate the mediation.

R-10.   Administrative Conference

At the request of any party or upon the AAA's own initiative, the AAA may conduct an administrative conference, in person or by telephone, with the parties and/or their representatives. The conference may address such issues as arbitrator selection, potential mediation of the dispute, potential exchange of information, a timetable for hearings, and any other administrative matters. There is no administrative fee for this service.

R-11.   Fixing of Locale

The parties may mutually agree on the locale where the arbitration is to be held. If any party requests that the hearing be held in a specific locale and the other party files no objection thereto within fifteen days after notice of the request has been sent to it by the AAA, the locale shall be the one requested. If a party objects to the locale requested by the other party, the AAA shall have the power to determine the locale, and its decision shall be final and binding.

R-12.   Qualifications of an Arbitrator

(a) Any neutral arbitrator appointed pursuant to §§ R-13, R-14, R-15, or E-5, or selected by mutual choice of the parties or their appointees, shall be subject to disqualification for the reasons specified in § R-19. If the parties specifically so agree in writing, the arbitrator shall not be subject to disqualification for those reasons.

(b) Unless the parties agree otherwise, an arbitrator selected unilaterally by one party is a party-appointed arbitrator and is not subject to disqualification pursuant to § R-19.

R-13.   Appointment from Panel

If the parties have not appointed an arbitrator and have not provided any other method of appointment, the arbitrator shall be appointed in the following manner:

(a) Immediately after the filing of the submission or the answering statement or the expiration of the time within which the answering statement is to be filed, the AAA shall send simultaneously to each party to the dispute an identical list of names of persons chosen from the panel. The parties are encouraged to agree to an arbitrator from the submitted list and to advise the AAA of their agreement.

(b) If the parties are unable to agree upon an arbitrator, each party to the dispute shall have fifteen days from the transmittal date in which to strike names objected to, number the remaining names in order of preference, and return the list to the AAA. If a party does not return the list within the time specified, all persons named therein shall be deemed acceptable. From among the persons who have been approved on both lists, and in accordance with the designated order of mutual preference, the AAA shall invite the acceptance of an arbitrator to serve. If the parties fail to agree on any of the persons named, or if acceptable arbitrators are unable to act, or if for any other reason the appointment cannot be made from the submitted lists, the AAA shall have the power to make the appointment from among other members of the panel without the submission of additional lists.

(c) Unless the parties have agreed otherwise no later than fifteen days after the commencement of an arbitration, if the notice of arbitration names two or more claimants or two or more respondents, the AAA shall appoint all the arbitrators.

R-14. Direct Appointment by a Party

(a) If the agreement of the parties names an arbitrator or specifies a method of appointing an arbitrator, that designation or method shall be followed. The notice of appointment, with the name and address of the arbitrator, shall be filed with the AAA by the appointing party. Upon the request of any appointing party, the AAA shall submit a list of members of.the panel from which the party may, if it so desires, make the appointment.

(b) If the agreement specifies a period of time within which an arbitrator shall be appointed and any party fails to make the appointment within that period, the AAA shall make the appointment.

(c) If no period of time is specified in the agreement, the AAA shall notify the party to make the appointment. If within fifteen days after such notice has been sent, an arbitrator has not been appointed by a party, the AAA shall make the appointment.

R-15. Appointment of Neutral Arbitrator by Party-Appointed Arbitrators or Parties

(a) If the parties have selected party-appointed arbitrators, or if such arbitrators have been appointed as provided in § R-14, and the parties have authorized them to appoint a neutral arbitrator within a specified time and no appointment is made within that time or any agreed extension, the AAA may appoint a neutral arbitrator, who shall act as chairperson.

(b) If no period of time is specified for appointment of the neutral arbitrator and the party-appointed arbitrators or the parties do not make the appointment within fifteen days from the date of the appointment of the last party-appointed arbitrator, the AAA may appoint the neutral arbitrator, who shall act as chairperson.

(c) If the parties have agreed that their party-appointed arbitrators shall appoint the neutral arbitrator from the panel, the AAA shall furnish to the party-appointed arbitrators, in the manner provided in § R-13, a list selected from the panel, and the appointment of the neutral arbitrator shall be made as provided in that section.

R-16. Nationality of Arbitrator

Where the parties are nationals or residents of different countries, the AAA, at the request of any party or on its own initiative, may appoint as a neutral arbitrator a national of a country other than that of any of the parties. The request must be made prior to the time set for the appointment of the arbitrator as agreed by the parties or set by these rules.

R-17. · Number of Arbitrators

If the arbitration agreement does not specify the number of arbitrators, the dispute shall be heard and determined by one arbitrator, unless the AAA, in its discretion, directs that three arbitrators be appointed. The parties may request three arbitrators in their demand or answer, which request the AAA will consider in exercising its discretion regarding the number of arbitrators appointed to the dispute.

R-18. Notice to Arbitrator of Appointment

Notice of the appointment of the neutral arbitrator, whether appointed mutually by the parties or by the AAA, shall be sent to the arbitrator by the AAA, together with a copy of these rules, and the signed acceptance of the arbitrator shall be filed with the AAA prior to the opening of the first hearing.

R-19. Disclosure and Challenge Procedure

(a) Any person appointed as a neutral arbitrator shall disclose to the AAA any circumstance likely to affect impartiality or independence, including any bias or any financial or personal interest in the result of the arbitration or any past or present relationship with the parties or their representatives. Upon receipt of such information from the arbitrator or another source, the AAA shall communicate the information to the parties and, if it deems it appropriate to do so, to the arbitrator and others.

(b) Upon objection of a party to the continued service of a neutral arbitrator, the AAA shall determine whether the arbitrator should be disqualified and shall inform the parties of its decision, which shall be conclusive.

R-20. Communication with Arbitrator

(a) No party and no one acting on behalf of any party shall communicate unilaterally concerning the arbitration with a neutral arbitrator or a candidate for neutral arbitrator. Unless the parties agree otherwise or the arbitrator so directs, any communication from the parties to a neutral arbitrator shall be sent to the AAA for transmittal to the arbitrator.

(b) The parties or the arbitrators may also agree that once the panel has been constituted, no party and no one acting on behalf of any party shall communicate unilaterally concerning the arbitration with any party-appointed arbitrator.

R-21. Vacancies

(a) If for any reason an arbitrator is unable to perform the duties of the office, the AAA may, on proof satisfactory to it, declare the office vacant. Vacancies shall be filled in accordance with the applicable provisions of these rules.

(b) In the event of a vacancy in a panel of neutral arbitrators after the hearings have commenced, the remaining arbitrator or arbitrators may continue with the hearing and determination of the controversy, unless the parties agree otherwise.

(c) In the event of the appointment of a substitute arbitrator, the panel of arbitrators shall determine in its sole discretion whether it is necessary to repeat all or part of any prior hearings.

R-22. Preliminary Hearing

(a) At the request of any party or at the discretion of the arbitrator or the AAA, the arbitrator may schedule as soon as practicable a preliminary hearing with the parties and/or their representatives. The preliminary hearing may be conducted by telephone at the arbitrator's discretion. There is no administrative fee for the first preliminary hearing.

(b) During the preliminary hearing, the parties and the arbitrator should discuss the future conduct of the case, including clarification of the issues and claims, a schedule for the hearings, and any other preliminary matters.

R-23. Exchange of Information

(a) At the request of any party or at the discretion of the arbitrator, consistent with the expedited nature of arbitration, the arbitrator may direct (i) the production of documents and other information, and (ii) the identification of any witnesses to be called.

(b) At least five business days prior to the hearing, the parties shall exchange copies of all exhibits they intend to submit at the hearing.

(c) The arbitrator is authorized to resolve any disputes concerning the exchange of information.

R-24. Date, Time, and Place of Hearing

The arbitrator shall set the date, time, and place for each hearing. The parties shall respond to requests for hearing dates in a timely manner, be cooperative in scheduling the earliest practicable date, and adhere to the established hearing schedule. The AAA shall send a notice of hearing to the parties at least ten days in advance of the hearing date, unless otherwise agreed by the parties.

R-25. Attendance at Hearings

The arbitrator and the AAA shall maintain the privacy of the hearings unless the law provides to the contrary. Any person having a direct interest in the arbitration is entitled to attend hearings. The arbitrator shall otherwise have the power to require the exclusion of any witness, other than a party or other essential person, during the testimony of any other witness. It shall be discretionary with the arbitrator to determine the propriety of the attendance of any other person other than a party and its representatives.

R-26. Representation

Any party may be represented by counsel or other authorized representative. A party intending to be so represented shall notify the other party and the AAA of the name and address of the representative at least three days prior to the date set for the hearing at which that person is first to appear. When such a representative initiates an arbitration or responds for a party, notice is deemed to have been given.

R-27. Oaths

Before proceeding with the first hearing, each arbitrator may take an oath of office and, if required by law, shall do so. The arbitrator may require witnesses to testify under oath administered by any duly qualified person and, if it is required by law or requested by any party, shall do so.

R-28. Stenographic Record

Any party desiring a stenographic record shall make arrangements directly with a stenographer and shall notify the other parties of these arrangements at least three days in advance of the hearing. The requesting party or parties shall pay the cost of the record. If the transcript is agreed to by the parties, or determined by the arbitrator to be the official record of the proceeding, it must be provided to the arbitrator and made available to the other parties for inspection, at a date, time, and place determined by the arbitrator.

R-29. Interpreters

Any party wishing an interpreter shall make all arrangements directly with the interpreter and shall assume the costs of the service.

R-30. Postponements

The arbitrator may postpone any hearing upon agreement of the parties, upon request of a party for good cause shown, or upon the arbitrator's own initiative. A party or parties causing a postponement of a hearing will be charged a postponement fee, as set forth in the administrative fee schedule.

R-31. Arbitration in the Absence of a Party or Representative

Unless the law provides to the contrary, the arbitration may proceed in the absence of any party or representative who, after due notice, fails to be present or fails to obtain a postponement. An award shall not be made solely on the default of a party. The arbitrator shall require the party who is present to submit such evidence as the arbitrator may require for the making of an award.

R-32. Conduct of Proceedings

(a) The claimant shall present evidence to support its claim. The respondent shall then present evidence to support its defense. Witnesses for each party shall also submit to questions from the arbitrator and the adverse party. The arbitrator has the discretion to vary this procedure, provided that the parties are treated with equality and that each party has the right to be heard and is given a fair opportunity to present its case.

(b) The arbitrator, exercising his or her discretion, shall conduct the proceedings with a view to expediting the resolution of the dispute and may direct the order of proof, bifurcate proceedings, and direct the parties to focus their presentations on issues the decision of which could dispose of all or part of the case.

(c) The parties may agree to waive oral hearings in any case.

R-33. Evidence

(a) The parties may offer such evidence as is relevant and material to the dispute and shall produce such evidence as the arbitrator may deem necessary to an understanding and determination of the dispute. Conformity to legal rules of evidence shall not be necessary. All evidence shall be taken in the presence of all of the arbitrators and all of the parties, except where any of the parties is absent, in default, or has waived the right to be present.

(b) The arbitrator shall determine the admissibility, relevance, and materiality of the evidence offered and may exclude evidence deemed by the arbitrator to be cumulative or irrelevant.

(c) The arbitrator shall take into account applicable principles of legal privilege, such as those involving the confidentiality of communications between a lawyer and client.

(d) An arbitrator or other person authorized by law to subpoena witnesses or documents may do so upon the request of any party or independently.

R-34. Evidence by Affidavit and Post-Hearing Filing of Documents or Other Evidence

(a) The arbitrator may receive and consider the evidence of witnesses by declaration or affidavit, but shall give it only such weight as the arbitrator deems it entitled to after consideration of any objection made to its admission.

(b) If the parties agree or the arbitrator directs that documents or other evidence be submitted to the arbitrator after the hearing, the documents or other evidence shall be filed with the AAA for transmission to the arbitrator. All parties shall be afforded an opportunity to examine and respond to such documents or other evidence.

R-35. Inspection or Investigation

An arbitrator finding it necessary to make an inspection or investigation in connection with the arbitration shall direct the AAA to so advise the parties. The arbitrator shall set the date and time and the AAA shall notify the parties. Any party who so desires may be present at such an inspection or investigation. In the event that one or all parties are not present at the inspection or investigation, the arbitrator shall make an oral or written report to the parties and afford them an opportunity to comment.

R-36. Interim Measures

(a) The arbitrator may take whatever interim measures he or she deems necessary, including injunctive relief and measures for the protection or conservation of property and disposition of perishable goods.

(b) Such interim measures may take the form of an interim award, and the arbitrator may require security for the costs of such measures.

(c) A request for interim measures addressed by a party to a judicial authority shall not be deemed incompatible with the agreement to arbitrate or a waiver of the right to arbitrate.

R-37. Closing of Hearing

The arbitrator shall specifically inquire of all parties whether they have any further proofs to offer or witnesses to be heard. Upon receiving negative replies or if satisfied that the record is complete, the arbitrator shall declare the hearing closed. If briefs are to be filed, the hearing shall be declared closed as of the final date set by the arbitrator for the receipt of briefs. If documents are to be filed as provided in § R-34 and the date set for their receipt is later than that set for the receipt of briefs, the later date shall be the closing date of the hearing. The time limit within which the arbitrator is required to make the award shall commence, in the absence of other agreements by the parties, upon the closing of the hearing.

R-38. Reopening of Hearing

The hearing may be reopened on the arbitrator's initiative, or upon application of a party, at any time before the award is made. If reopening the hearing would prevent the making of the award within the specific time agreed on by the parties in the contract(s) out of which the controversy has arisen, the matter may not be reopened unless the parties agree on an extension of time. When no specific date is fixed in the contract, the arbitrator may reopen the hearing and shall have thirty days from the closing of the reopened hearing within which to make an award.

R-39. Waiver of Rules

Any party who proceeds with the arbitration after knowledge that any provision or requirement of these rules has not been complied with and who fails to state an objection in writing shall be deemed to have waived the right to object.

R-40. Extensions of Time

The parties may modify any period of time by mutual agreement. The AAA or the arbitrator may for good cause extend any period of time established by these rules, except the time for making the award. The AAA shall notify the parties of any extension.

R-41. Serving of Notice

(a) Any papers, notices, or process necessary or proper for the initiation or continuation of an arbitration under these rules, for any court action in connection therewith, or for the entry of judgment on any award made under these rules may be served on a party by mail addressed to the party, or its representative at the last known address or by personal service, in or outside the state where the arbitration is to be held, provided that reasonable opportunity to be heard with regard to the dispute is or has been granted to the party.

(b) The AAA, the arbitrator, and the parties may also use overnight delivery or electronic facsimile transmission (fax), to give the notices required by these rules. Where all parties and the arbitrator agree, notices may be transmitted by electronic mail (E-mail), or other methods of communication.

(c) Unless otherwise instructed by the AAA or by the arbitrator, any documents submitted by any party to the AAA or to the arbitrator shall simultaneously be provided to the other party or parties to the arbitration.

R-42. Majority Decision
When the panel consists of more than one arbitrator, unless required by law or by the arbitration agreement, a majority of the arbitrators must make all decisions.

R-43. Time of Award
The award shall be made promptly by the arbitrator and, unless otherwise agreed by the parties or specified by law, no later than thirty days from the date of closing the hearing, or, if oral hearings have been waived, from the date of the AAA's transmittal of the final statements and proofs to the arbitrator.

R-44. Form of Award
(a) Any award shall be in writing and signed by a majority of the arbitrators. It shall be executed in the manner required by law.

(b) The arbitrator need not render a reasoned award unless the parties request such an award in writing prior to appointment of the arbitrator or unless the arbitrator determines that a reasoned award is appropriate.

R-45. Scope of Award
(a) The arbitrator may grant any remedy or relief that the arbitrator deems just and equitable and within the scope of the agreement of the parties, including, but not limited to, specific performance of a contract.

(b) In addition to a final award, the arbitrator may make other decisions, including interim, interlocutory, or partial rulings, orders, and awards. In any interim, interlocutory, or partial award, the arbitrator may assess and apportion the fees, expenses, and compensation related to such award as the arbitrator determines is appropriate.

(c) In the final award, the arbitrator shall assess the fees, expenses, and compensation provided in §§ R-51, R-52, and R-53. The arbitrator may apportion such fees, expenses, and compensation among the parties in such amounts as the arbitrator determines is appropriate.

(d) The award of the arbitrator(s) may include: (a) interest at such rate and from such date as the arbitrator(s) may deem appropriate; and (b) an award of

attorneys' fees if all parties have requested such an award or it is authorized
by law or their arbitration agreement.

R-46.   Award upon Settlement

If the parties settle their dispute during the course of the arbitration and if the
parties so request, the arbitrator may set forth the terms of the settlement in a
"consent award."

R-47.   Delivery of Award to Parties

Parties shall accept as notice and delivery of the award the placing of the award
or a true copy thereof in the mail addressed to the parties or their representatives
at the last known addresses, personal or electronic service of the award, or the
filing of the award in any other manner that is permitted by law.

R-48.   Modification of Award

Within twenty days after the transmittal of an award, any party, upon notice to
the other parties, may request the arbitrator, through the AAA, to correct any
clerical, typographical, or computational errors in the award. The arbitrator is not
empowered to redetermine the merits of any claim already decided. The other
parties shall be given ten days to respond to the request. The arbitrator shall
dispose of the request within twenty days after transmittal by the AAA to the
arbitrator of the request and any response thereto.

R-49.   Release of Documents for Judicial Proceedings

The AAA shall, upon the written request of a party, furnish to the party, at the
party's expense, certified copies of any papers in the AAA's possession that may
be required in judicial proceedings relating to the arbitration.

R-50.   Applications to Court and Exclusion of Liability

- (a) No judicial proceeding by a party relating to the subject matter of the
  arbitration shall be deemed a waiver of the party's right to arbitrate.
- (b) Neither the AAA nor any arbitrator in a proceeding under these rules is a
  necessary party in judicial proceedings relating to the arbitration.
- (c) Parties to an arbitration under these rules shall be deemed to have
  consented that judgment upon the arbitration award may be entered in any
  federal or state court having jurisdiction thereof.
- (d) Neither the AAA nor any arbitrator shall be liable to any party for any act
  or omission in connection with any arbitration conducted under these rules.

R-51.   Administrative Fees

As a not-for-profit organization, the AAA shall prescribe filing and other
administrative fees and service charges to compensate it for the cost of providing
administrative services. The fees in effect when the fee or charge is incurred shall
be applicable.

The filing fee shall be advanced by the party or parties making a claim or counterclaim, subject to final apportionment by the arbitrator in the award. The AAA may, in the event of extreme hardship on the part of any party, defer or reduce the administrative fees.

R-52. Expenses

The expenses of witnesses for either side shall be paid by the party producing such witnesses. All other expenses of the arbitration, including required travel and other expenses of the arbitrator, AAA representatives, and any witness and the cost of any proof produced at the direct request of the arbitrator, shall be borne equally by the parties, unless they agree otherwise or unless the arbitrator in the award assesses such expenses or any part thereof against any specified party or parties.

R-53. Neutral Arbitrator's Compensation

(a) Unless the parties agree otherwise, members of the National Panel of Commercial Arbitrators appointed as neutrals on cases administered under the Expedited Procedures with claims not exceeding $10,000, will customarily serve without compensation for the first day of service. Thereafter, arbitrators shall receive compensation as set forth herein.

(b) Arbitrators shall be compensated at a rate consistent with the arbitrator's stated rate of compensation, beginning with the first day of hearing in all cases with claims exceeding $10,000.

(c) If there is disagreement concerning the terms of compensation, an appropriate rate shall be established with the arbitrator by the AAA and confirmed to the parties.

(d) Any arrangement for the compensation of a neutral arbitrator shall be made through the AAA and not directly between the parties and the arbitrator.

R-54. Deposits

The AAA may require the parties to deposit in advance of any hearings such sums of money as it deems necessary to cover the expense of the arbitration, including the arbitrator's fee, if any, and shall render an accounting to the parties and return any unexpended balance at the conclusion of the case.

R-55. Interpretation and Application of Rules

The arbitrator shall interpret and apply these rules insofar as they relate to the arbitrator's powers and duties. When there is more than one arbitrator and a difference arises among them concerning the meaning or application of these rules, it shall be decided by a majority vote. If that is not possible, either an arbitrator or a party may refer the question to the AAA for final decision. All other rules shall be interpreted and applied by the AAA.

R-56. Suspension for Nonpayment

If arbitrator compensation or administrative charges have not been paid in full, the AAA may so inform the parties in order that one of them may advance the required payment. If such payments are not made, the arbitrator may order the suspension or termination of the proceedings. If no arbitrator has yet been appointed, the AAA may suspend the proceedings.

Appendix 7:

Insurance Contract

**HOMEOWNERS 6
UNIT-OWNERS FORM**

AGREEMENT

We will provide the insurance described in this policy in return for the premium and compliance with all applicable provisions of this policy.

DEFINITIONS

In this policy, "you" and "your" refer to the "named insured" shown in the Declarations and the spouse if a resident of the same household. "We," "us" and "our" refer to the Company providing this insurance. In addition, certain words and phrases are defined as follows:

1. "Bodily injury" means bodily harm, sickness or disease, including required care, loss of services and death that results.

2. "Business" includes trade, profession or occupation.

3. "Insured" means you and residents of your household who are:

   a. Your relatives; or

   b. Other persons under the age of 21 and in the care of any person named above.

   Under Section II, "insured" also means:

   c. With respect to animals or watercraft to which this policy applies, any person or organization legally responsible for these animals or watercraft which are owned by you or any person included in **3.a.** or **3.b.** above. A person or organization using or having custody of these animals or watercraft in the course of any "business" or without consent of the owner is not an "insured";

   d. With respect to any vehicle to which this policy applies:

      (1) Persons while engaged in your employ or that of any person included in **3.a.** or **3.b.** above; or

      (2) Other persons using the vehicle on an "insured location" with your consent.

4. "Insured location" means:

   a. The "residence premises";

   b. The part of other premises, other structures and grounds used by you as a residence and:

      (1) Which is shown in the Declarations; or

      (2) Which is acquired by you during the policy period for your use as a residence;

   c. Any premises used by you in connection with a premises in **4.a.** and **4.b.** above;

   d. Any part of a premises:

      (1) Not owned by an "insured"; and

      (2) Where an "insured" is temporarily residing;

   e. Vacant land, other than farm land, owned by or rented to an "insured";

   f. Land owned by or rented to an "insured" on which a one or two family dwelling is being built as a residence for an "insured";

   g. Individual or family cemetery plots or burial vaults of an "insured"; or

   h. Any part of a premises occasionally rented to an "insured" for other than "business" use.

5. "Occurrence" means an accident, including continuous or repeated exposure to substantially the same general harmful conditions, which results, during the policy period, in:

   a. "Bodily injury"; or

   b. "Property damage."

6. "Property damage" means physical injury to, destruction of, or loss of use of tangible property.

7. "Residence employee" means:

   a. An employee of an "insured" whose duties are related to the maintenance or use of the "residence premises," including household or domestic services; or

   b. One who performs similar duties elsewhere not related to the "business" of an "insured."

8. "Residence premises" means the unit where you reside shown as the "residence premises" in the Declarations.

SECTION I – PROPERTY COVERAGES

COVERAGE A – Dwelling

We cover:

1. The alterations, appliances, fixtures and improvements which are part of the building contained within the "residence premises";
2. Items of real property which pertain exclusively to the "residence premises";
3. Property which is your insurance responsibility under a corporation or association of property owners agreement; or
4. Structures owned solely by you, other than the "residence premises," at the location of the "residence premises."

This coverage does not apply to land, including land on which the "residence premises," real property or structures are located.

We do not cover:

1. Structures used in whole or in part for "business" purposes; or
2. Structures rented or held for rental to any person not a tenant of the "residence premises," unless used solely as a private garage.

COVERAGE C – Personal Property

We cover personal property owned or used by an "insured" while it is anywhere in the world. At your request, we will cover personal property owned by:

1. Others while the property is on the part of the "residence premises" occupied by an "insured";
2. A guest or a "residence employee," while the property is in any residence occupied by an "insured."

Our limit of liability for personal property usually located at an "insured's" residence, other than the "residence premises," is 10% of the limit of liability for Coverage C, or $1000, whichever is greater. Personal property in a newly acquired principal residence is not subject to this limitation for the 30 days from the time you begin to move the property there.

Special Limits of Liability. These limits do not increase the Coverage C limit of liability. The special limit for each numbered category below is the total limit for each loss for all property in that category.

1. $200 on money, bank notes, bullion, gold other than goldware, silver other than silverware, platinum, coins and medals.

2. $1000 on securities, accounts, deeds, evidences of debt, letters of credit, notes other than bank notes, manuscripts, personal records, passports, tickets and stamps. This dollar limit applies to these categories regardless of the medium (such as paper or computer software) on which the material exists.

   This limit includes the cost to research, replace or restore the information from the lost or damaged material.

3. $1000 on watercraft, including their trailers, furnishings, equipment and outboard engines or motors.

4. $1000 on trailers not used with watercraft.

5. $1000 for loss by theft of jewelry, watches, furs, precious and semi-precious stones.

6. $2000 for loss by theft of firearms.

7. $2500 for loss by theft of silverware, silver-plated ware, goldware, gold-plated ware and pewterware. This includes flatware, hollowware, tea sets, trays and trophies made of or including silver, gold or pewter.

8. $2500 on property, on the "residence premises," used at any time or in any manner for any "business" purpose.

9. $250 on property, away from the "residence premises," used at any time or in any manner for any "business" purpose. However, this limit does not apply to loss to adaptable electronic apparatus as described in Special Limits **10.** and **11.** below.

10. $1000 for loss to electronic apparatus, while in or upon a motor vehicle or other motorized land conveyance, if the electronic apparatus is equipped to be operated by power from the electrical system of the vehicle or conveyance while retaining its capability of being operated by other sources of power. Electronic apparatus includes:

    a. Accessories or antennas; or

    b. Tapes, wires, records, discs or other media;

    for use with any electronic apparatus.

11. $1000 for loss to electronic apparatus, while not in or upon a motor vehicle or other motorized land conveyance, if the electronic apparatus:

a. Is equipped to be operated by power from the electrical system of the vehicle or conveyance while retaining its capability of being operated by other sources of power;

b. Is away from the "residence premises"; and

c. Is used at any time or in any manner for any "business" purpose.

Electronic apparatus includes:

a. Accessories or antennas; or

b. Tapes, wires, records, discs or other media;

for use with any electronic apparatus.

Property Not Covered. We do not cover:

1. Articles separately described and specifically insured in this or other insurance;

2. Animals, birds or fish;

3. Motor vehicles or all other motorized land conveyances. This includes:

a. Their equipment and accessories; or

b. Electronic apparatus that is designed to be operated solely by use of the power from the electrical system of motor vehicles or all other motorized land conveyances. Electronic apparatus includes:

(1) Accessories or antennas; or

(2) Tapes, wires, records, discs or other media

for use with any electronic apparatus.

The exclusion of property described in **3.a.** and **3.b.** above applies only while the property is in or upon the vehicle or conveyance.

We do cover vehicles or conveyances not subject to motor vehicle registration which are:

a. Used to service an "insured's" residence; or

b. Designed for assisting the handicapped;

4. Aircraft and parts. Aircraft means any contrivance used or designed for flight, except model or hobby aircraft not used or designed to carry people or cargo;

5. Property of roomers, boarders and other tenants, except property of roomers and boarders related to an "insured";

6. Property in an apartment regularly rented or held for rental to others by an "insured";

7. Property rented or held for rental to others off the "residence premises";

8. "Business" data, including such data stored in:

a. Books of account, drawings or other paper records; or

b. Electronic data processing tapes, wires, records, discs or other software media.

However, we do cover the cost of blank recording or storage media, and of pre-recorded computer programs available on the retail market; or

9. Credit cards or fund transfer cards except as provided in Additional Coverages 6.

COVERAGE D – Loss Of Use

The limit of liability for Coverage D is the total limit for all the coverages that follow.

1. If a loss by a Peril Insured Against under this policy to covered property or the building containing the property, makes the "residence premises" not fit to live in, we cover, at your choice, either of the following. However, if the "residence premises" is not your principal place of residence, we will not provide the option under paragraph b. below.

a. **Additional Living Expense,** meaning any necessary increase in living expenses incurred by you so that your household can maintain its normal standard of living; or

b. **Fair Rental Value,** meaning the fair rental value of that part of the "residence premises" where you reside less any expenses that do not continue while the premises is not fit to live in.

Payment under a. or b. will be for the shortest time required to repair or replace the damage or, if you permanently relocate, the shortest time required for your household to settle elsewhere.

2. If a loss covered under this Section makes that part of the "residence premises" rented to others or held for rental by you not fit to live in, we cover the:

Fair Rental Value, meaning the fair rental value of that part of the "residence premises" rented to others or held for rental by you less any expenses that do not continue while the premises is not fit to live in.

Payment will be for the shortest time required to repair or replace that part of the premises rented or held for rental.

3. If a civil authority prohibits you from use of the "residence premises" as a result of direct damage to neighboring premises by a Peril Insured Against in this policy, we cover the Additional Living Expense and Fair Rental Value loss as provided under **1.** and **2.** above for no more than two weeks.

The periods of time under **1.**, **2.** and **3.** above are not limited by expiration of this policy.

We do not cover loss or expense due to cancellation of a lease or agreement.

ADDITIONAL COVERAGES

1. **Debris Removal.** We will pay your reasonable expense for the removal of:

   a. Debris of covered property if a Peril Insured Against that applies to the damaged property causes the loss; or

   b. Ash, dust or particles from a volcanic eruption that has caused direct loss to a building or property contained in a building.

   This expense is included in the limit of liability that applies to the damaged property. If the amount to be paid for the actual damage to the property plus the debris removal expense is more than the limit of liability for the damaged property, an additional 5% of that limit of liability is available for debris removal expense.

   We will also pay your reasonable expense, up to $500, for the removal from the "residence premises" of:

   a. Your tree(s) felled by the peril of Windstorm or Hail;

   b. Your tree(s) felled by the peril of Weight of Ice, Snow or Sleet; or

   c. A neighbor's tree(s) felled by a Peril Insured Against under Coverage C;

   provided the tree(s) damages a covered structure. The $500 limit is the most we will pay in any one loss regardless of the number of fallen trees.

2. **Reasonable Repairs.** In the event that covered property is damaged by an applicable Peril Insured Against, we will pay the reasonable cost incurred by you for necessary measures taken solely to protect against further damage. If the measures taken involve repair to other damaged property, we will pay for those measures only if that property is covered under this policy and the damage to that property is caused by an applicable Peril Insured Against.

This coverage:

   a. Does not increase the limit of liability that applies to the covered property;

   b. Does not relieve you of your duties, in case of a loss to covered property, as set forth in SECTION I – CONDITION **2.d.**

3. **Trees, Shrubs and Other Plants.** We cover trees, shrubs, plants or lawns, on the "residence premises," for loss caused by the following Perils Insured Against: Fire or lightning, Explosion, Riot or civil commotion, Aircraft, Vehicles not owned or operated by a resident of the "residence premises," Vandalism or malicious mischief or Theft.

   We will pay up to 10% of the limit of liability that applies to Coverage C for all trees, shrubs, plants or lawns. No more than $500 of this limit will be available for any one tree, shrub or plant. We do not cover property grown for "business" purposes.

   This coverage is additional insurance.

4. **Fire Department Service Charge.** We will pay up to $500 for your liability assumed by contract or agreement for fire department charges incurred when the fire department is called to save or protect covered property from a Peril Insured Against. We do not cover fire department service charges if the property is located within the limits of the city, municipality or protection district furnishing the fire department response.

   This coverage is additional insurance. No deductible applies to this coverage.

5. **Property Removed.** We insure covered property against direct loss from any cause while being removed from a premises endangered by a Peril Insured Against and for no more than 30 days while removed. This coverage does not change the limit of liability that applies to the property being removed.

6. **Credit Card, Fund Transfer Card, Forgery and Counterfeit Money.**

   We will pay up to $500 for:

   a. The legal obligation of an "insured" to pay because of the theft or unauthorized use of credit cards issued to or registered in an "insured's" name;

   b. Loss resulting from theft or unauthorized use of a fund transfer card used for deposit, withdrawal or transfer of funds, issued to or registered in an "insured's" name;

c. Loss to an "insured" caused by forgery or alteration of any check or negotiable instrument; and

d. Loss to an "insured" through acceptance in good faith of counterfeit United States or Canadian paper currency.

We do not cover use of a credit card or fund transfer card:

a. By a resident of your household;

b. By a person who has been entrusted with either type of card; or

c. If an "insured" has not complied with all terms and conditions under which the cards are issued.

All loss resulting from a series of acts committed by any one person or in which any one person is concerned or implicated is considered to be one loss.

We do not cover loss arising out of "business" use or dishonesty of an "insured."

This coverage is additional insurance. No deductible applies to this coverage.

Defense:

a. We may investigate and settle any claim or suit that we decide is appropriate. Our duty to defend a claim or suit ends when the amount we pay for the loss equals our limit of liability.

b. If a suit is brought against an "insured" for liability under the Credit Card or Fund Transfer Card coverage, we will provide a defense at our expense by counsel of our choice.

c. We have the option to defend at our expense an "insured" or an "insured's" bank against any suit for the enforcement of payment under the Forgery coverage.

7. **Loss Assessment.** We will pay up to $1000 for your share of loss assessment charged during the policy period against you by a corporation or association of property owners, when the assessment is made as a result of direct loss to the property, owned by all members collectively, caused by a Peril Insured Against under COVERAGE A – DWELLING, other than earthquake or land shock waves or tremors before, during or after a volcanic eruption.

This coverage applies only to loss assessments charged against you as owner or tenant of the "residence premises."

We do not cover loss assessments charged against you or a corporation or association of property owners by any governmental body.

The limit of $1000 is the most we will pay with respect to any one loss, regardless of the number of assessments.

Condition 1. Policy Period, under SECTIONS I and II CONDITIONS, does not apply to this coverage.

8. **Collapse.** We insure for direct physical loss to covered property involving collapse of a building or any part of a building caused only by one or more of the following:

a. Perils Insured Against in COVERAGE C – PERSONAL PROPERTY. These perils apply to covered buildings and personal property for loss insured by this additional coverage;

b. Hidden decay;

c. Hidden insect or vermin damage;

d. Weight of contents, equipment, animals or people;

e. Weight of rain which collects on a roof; or

f. Use of defective material or methods in construction, remodeling or renovation if the collapse occurs during the course of the construction, remodeling or renovation.

Loss to an awning, fence, patio, pavement, swimming pool, underground pipe, flue, drain, cesspool, septic tank, foundation, retaining wall, bulkhead, pier, wharf or dock is not included under items **b., c., d., e.,** and **f.** unless the loss is a direct result of the collapse of a building.

Collapse does not include settling, cracking, shrinking, bulging or expansion.

This coverage does not increase the limit of liability applying to the damaged covered property.

9. **Glass or Safety Glazing Material**

We cover:

a. The breakage of glass or safety glazing material which is part of a building, storm door or storm window, and covered under Coverage A; and

b. Damage to covered property by glass or safety glazing material which is part of a building, storm door or storm window.

This coverage does not include loss on the "residence premises" if the dwelling has been vacant for more than 30 consecutive days immediately before the loss. A dwelling being constructed is not considered vacant.

Loss for damage to glass will be settled on the basis of replacement with safety glazing materials when required by ordinance or law.

This coverage does not increase the limit of liability that applies to the damaged property.

SECTION I – PERILS INSURED AGAINST

We insure for direct physical loss to the property described in Coverages A and C caused by a peril listed below unless the loss is excluded in SECTION I – EXCLUSIONS.

1. Fire or lightning.

2. Windstorm or hail.

This peril does not include loss to the inside of a building or the property contained in a building caused by rain, snow, sleet, sand or dust unless the direct force of wind or hail damages the building causing an opening in a roof or a wall and the rain, snow, sleet, sand or dust enters through this opening.

This peril includes loss to watercraft and their trailers, furnishings, equipment, and outboard engines or motors, only while inside a fully enclosed building.

3. Explosion.

4. Riot or civil commotion.

5. Aircraft, including self-propelled missiles and spacecraft.

6. Vehicles.

This peril does not include loss to a fence, driveway or walk caused by a vehicle owned or operated by a resident of the "residence premises."

7. Smoke, meaning sudden and accidental damage from smoke.

This peril does not include loss caused by smoke from agricultural smudging or industrial operations.

8. Vandalism or malicious mischief.

This peril does not include loss to property on the "residence premises" if the dwelling has been vacant for more than 30 consecutive days immediately before the loss. A dwelling being constructed is not considered vacant.

9. Theft, including attempted theft and loss of property from a known place when it is likely that the property has been stolen.

This peril does not include loss caused by theft:

a. Committed by an "insured";

b. In or to a dwelling under construction, or of materials and supplies for use in the construction until the dwelling is finished and occupied; or

c. From that part of a "residence premises" rented by an "insured" to other than an "insured."

This peril does not include loss caused by theft that occurs off the "residence premises" of:

a. Property while at any other residence owned by, rented to, or occupied by an "insured," except while an "insured" is temporarily living there. Property of a student who is an "insured" is covered while at a residence away from home if the student has been there at any time during the 45 days immediately before the loss;

b. Watercraft, and their furnishings, equipment and outboard engines or motors; or

c. Trailers and campers.

10. Falling objects.

This peril does not include loss to the inside of a building or property contained in the building unless the roof or an outside wall of the building is first damaged by a falling object. Damage to the falling object itself is not included.

11. Weight of ice, snow or sleet which causes damage to a building or property contained in the building.

This peril does not include loss to an awning, fence, patio, pavement, swimming pool, foundation, retaining wall, bulkhead, pier, wharf, or dock.

12. Accidental discharge or overflow of water or steam from within a plumbing, heating, air conditioning or automatic fire protective sprinkler system or from within a household appliance. We also pay for tearing out and replacing any part of the building which is covered under Coverage A and on the "residence premises," if necessary to repair the system or appliance from which the water or steam escaped.

This peril does not include loss:

a. On the "residence premises," if the dwelling has been vacant for more than 30 consecutive days immediately before the loss. A dwelling being constructed is not considered vacant;

b. To the system or appliance from which the water or steam escaped;

c. Caused by or resulting from freezing except as provided in the peril of freezing below; or

d. On the "residence premises" caused by accidental discharge or overflow which occurs away from the building where the "residence premises" is located.

In this peril, a plumbing system does not include a sump, sump pump or related equipment.

13. Sudden and accidental tearing apart, cracking, burning or bulging of a steam or hot water heating system, an air conditioning or automatic fire protective sprinkler system, or an appliance for heating water.

This peril does not include loss caused by or resulting from freezing except as provided in the peril of freezing below.

14. Freezing of a plumbing, heating, air conditioning or automatic fire protective sprinkler system or of a household appliance.

This peril does not include loss on the "residence premises" while unoccupied, unless you have used reasonable care to:

a. Maintain heat in the building; or

b. Shut off the water supply and drain the system and appliances of water.

15. Sudden and accidental damage from artificially generated electrical current.

This peril does not include loss to a tube, transistor or similar electronic component.

16. Volcanic eruption other than loss caused by earthquake, land shock waves or tremors.

SECTION I – EXCLUSIONS

We do not insure for loss caused directly or indirectly by any of the following. Such loss is excluded regardless of any other cause or event contributing concurrently or in any sequence to the loss.

1. **Ordinance or Law,** meaning enforcement of any ordinance or law regulating the construction, repair, or demolition of a building or other structure, unless specifically provided under this policy.

2. **Earth Movement,** meaning earthquake including land shock waves or tremors before, during or after a volcanic eruption; landslide; mine subsidence; mudflow; earth sinking, rising or shifting; unless direct loss by:

   a. Fire;

   b. Explosion; or

   c. Breakage of glass or safety glazing material which is part of a building, storm door or storm window;

   ensues and then we will pay only for the ensuing loss.

   This exclusion does not apply to loss by theft.

3. **Water Damage,** meaning:

   a. Flood, surface water, waves, tidal water, overflow of a body of water, or spray from any of these, whether or not driven by wind;

   b. Water which backs up through sewers or drains or which overflows from a sump; or

   c. Water below the surface of the ground, including water which exerts pressure on or seeps or leaks through a building, sidewalk, driveway, foundation, swimming pool or other structure.

   Direct loss by fire, explosion or theft resulting from water damage is covered.

4. **Power Failure,** meaning the failure of power or other utility service if the failure takes place off the "residence premises." But, if a Peril Insured Against ensues on the "residence premises," we will pay only for that ensuing loss.

5. **Neglect,** meaning neglect of the "insured" to use all reasonable means to save and preserve property at and after the time of a loss.

6. **War,** including the following and any consequence of any of the following:

   a. Undeclared war, civil war, insurrection, rebellion or revolution;

   b. Warlike act by a military force or military personnel; or

   c. Destruction, seizure or use for a military purpose.

   Discharge of a nuclear weapon will be deemed a warlike act even if accidental.

7. **Nuclear Hazard,** to the extent set forth in the Nuclear Hazard Clause of SECTION I – CONDITIONS.

8. **Intentional Loss,** meaning any loss arising out of any act committed:

   a. By or at the direction of an "insured"; and

   b. With the intent to cause a loss.

SECTION I – CONDITIONS

1. **Insurable Interest and Limit of Liability.** Even if more than one person has an insurable interest in the property covered, we will not be liable in any one loss:

   a. To the "insured" for more than the amount of the "insured's" interest at the time of loss; or

   b. For more than the applicable limit of liability.

2. **Your Duties After Loss.** In case of a loss to covered property, you must see that the following are done:

   a. Give prompt notice to us or our agent;

   b. Notify the police in case of loss by theft;

   c. Notify the credit card or fund transfer card company in case of loss under Credit Card or Fund Transfer Card coverage;

   d. Protect the property from further damage. If repairs to the property are required, you must:

      (1) Make reasonable and necessary repairs to protect the property; and

      (2) Keep an accurate record of repair expenses;

   e. Prepare an inventory of damaged personal property showing the quantity, description, actual cash value and amount of loss. Attach all bills, receipts and related documents that justify the figures in the inventory;

   f. As often as we reasonably require:

      (1) Show the damaged property;

      (2) Provide us with records and documents we request and permit us to make copies; and

      (3) Submit to examination under oath, while not in the presence of any other "insured," and sign the same;

   g. Send to us, within 60 days after our request, your signed, sworn proof of loss which sets forth, to the best of your knowledge and belief:

      (1) The time and cause of loss;

      (2) The interest of the "insured" and all others in the property involved and all liens on the property;

      (3) Other insurance which may cover the loss;

      (4) Changes in title or occupancy of the property during the term of the policy;

      (5) Specifications of damaged buildings and detailed repair estimates;

   (6) The inventory of damaged personal property described in **2.e.** above;

   (7) Receipts for additional living expenses incurred and records that support the fair rental value loss; and

   (8) Evidence or affidavit that supports a claim under the Credit Card, Fund Transfer Card, Forgery and Counterfeit Money coverage, stating the amount and cause of loss.

3. **Loss Settlement.** Covered property losses are settled as follows:

   a. Personal property at actual cash value at the time of loss but not more than the amount required to repair or replace.

   b. Coverage A – Dwelling:

      (1) If the damage is repaired or replaced within a reasonable time, at the actual cost to repair or replace;

      (2) If the damage is not repaired or replaced, at actual cash value but not more than the amount required to repair or replace.

4. **Loss to a Pair or Set.** In case of loss to a pair or set we may elect to:

   a. Repair or replace any part to restore the pair or set to its value before the loss; or

   b. Pay the difference between actual cash value of the property before and after the loss.

5. **Glass Replacement.** Loss for damage to glass caused by a Peril Insured Against will be settled on the basis of replacement with safety glazing materials when required by ordinance or law.

6. **Appraisal.** If you and we fail to agree on the amount of loss, either may demand an appraisal of the loss. In this event, each party will choose a competent appraiser within 20 days after receiving a written request from the other. The two appraisers will choose an umpire. If they cannot agree upon an umpire within 15 days, you or we may request that the choice be made by a judge of a court of record in the state where the "residence premises" is located. The appraisers will separately set the amount of loss. If the appraisers submit a written report of an agreement to us, the amount agreed upon will be the amount of loss. If they fail to agree, they will submit their differences to the umpire. A decision agreed to by any two will set the amount of loss.

Each party will:

a. Pay its own appraiser; and

b. Bear the other expenses of the appraisal and umpire equally.

7. **Other Insurance.** If a loss covered by this policy is also covered by other insurance, except insurance in the name of a corporation or association of property owners, we will pay only the proportion of the loss that the limit of liability that applies under this policy bears to the total amount of insurance covering the loss.

If, at the time of loss, there is other insurance in the name of a corporation or association of property owners covering the same property covered by this policy, this insurance will be excess over the amount recoverable under such other insurance.

8. **Suit Against Us.** No action can be brought unless the policy provisions have been complied with and the action is started within one year after the date of loss.

9. **Our Option.** If we give you written notice within 30 days after we receive your signed, sworn proof of loss, we may repair or replace any part of the damaged property with like property.

10. **Loss Payment.** We will adjust all losses with you. We will pay you unless some other person is named in the policy or is legally entitled to receive payment. Loss will be payable 60 days after we receive your proof of loss and:

a. Reach an agreement with you;

b. There is an entry of a final judgment; or

c. There is a filing of an appraisal award with us.

11. **Abandonment of Property.** We need not accept any property abandoned by an "insured."

12. **Mortgage Clause.**

The word "mortgagee" includes trustee.

If a mortgagee is named in this policy, any loss payable under Coverage A – Dwelling will be paid to the mortgagee and you, as interests appear. If more than one mortgagee is named, the order of payment will be the same as the order of precedence of the mortgages.

If we deny your claim, that denial will not apply to a valid claim of the mortgagee, if the mortgagee:

a. Notifies us of any change in ownership, occupancy or substantial change in risk of which the mortgagee is aware;

b. Pays any premium due under this policy on demand if you have neglected to pay the premium; and

c. Submits a signed, sworn statement of loss within 60 days after receiving notice from us of your failure to do so. Policy conditions relating to Appraisal, Suit Against Us and Loss Payment apply to the mortgagee.

If we decide to cancel or not to renew this policy, the mortgagee will be notified at least 10 days before the date cancellation or nonrenewal takes effect.

If we pay the mortgagee for any loss and deny payment to you:

a. We are subrogated to all the rights of the mortgagee granted under the mortgage on the property; or

b. At our option, we may pay to the mortgagee the whole principal on the mortgage plus any accrued interest. In this event, we will receive a full assignment and transfer of the mortgage and all securities held as collateral to the mortgage debt.

Subrogation will not impair the right of the mortgagee to recover the full amount of the mortgagee's claim.

13. **No Benefit to Bailee.** We will not recognize any assignment or grant any coverage that benefits a person or organization holding, storing or moving property for a fee regardless of any other provision of this policy.

14. **Nuclear Hazard Clause.**

a. "Nuclear Hazard" means any nuclear reaction, radiation, or radioactive contamination, all whether controlled or uncontrolled or however caused, or any consequence of any of these.

b. Loss caused by the nuclear hazard will not be considered loss caused by fire, explosion, or smoke, whether these perils are specifically named in or otherwise included within the Perils Insured Against in Section I.

c. This policy does not apply under Section I to loss caused directly or indirectly by nuclear hazard, except that direct loss by fire resulting from the nuclear hazard is covered.

15. **Recovered Property.** If you or we recover any property for which we have made payment under this policy, you or we will notify the other of the recovery. At your option, the property will be returned to or retained by you or it will become our property. If the recovered property is returned to or retained by you, the loss payment will be adjusted based on the amount you received for the recovered property.

16. **Volcanic Eruption Period.** One or more volcanic eruptions that occur within a 72-hour period will be considered as one volcanic eruption.

SECTION II – LIABILITY COVERAGES

COVERAGE E – Personal Liability

If a claim is made or a suit is brought against an "insured" for damages because of "bodily injury" or "property damage" caused by an "occurrence" to which this coverage applies, we will:

1. Pay up to our limit of liability for the damages for which the "insured" is legally liable. Damages include prejudgment interest awarded against the "insured"; and

2. Provide a defense at our expense by counsel of our choice, even if the suit is groundless, false or fraudulent. We may investigate and settle any claim or suit that we decide is appropriate. Our duty to settle or defend ends when the amount we pay for damages resulting from the "occurrence" equals our limit of liability.

COVERAGE F – Medical Payments To Others

We will pay the necessary medical expenses that are incurred or medically ascertained within three years from the date of an accident causing "bodily injury." Medical expenses means reasonable charges for medical, surgical, x-ray, dental, ambulance, hospital, professional nursing, prosthetic devices and funeral services. This coverage does not apply to you or regular residents of your household except "residence employees." As to others, this coverage applies only:

1. To a person on the "insured location" with the permission of an "insured"; or

2. To a person off the "insured location," if the "bodily injury":

   a. Arises out of a condition on the "insured location" or the ways immediately adjoining;

   b. Is caused by the activities of an "insured";

   c. Is caused by a "residence employee" in the course of the "residence employee's" employment by an "insured"; or

   d. Is caused by an animal owned by or in the care of an "insured."

SECTION II – EXCLUSIONS

1. Coverage E – **Personal Liability** and **Coverage F – Medical Payments to Others** do not apply to "bodily injury" or "property damage":

   a. Which is expected or intended by the "insured";

   b. Arising out of or in connection with a "business" engaged in by an "insured." This exclusion applies but is not limited to an act or omission, regardless of its nature or circumstance, involving a service or duty rendered, promised, owed, or implied to be provided because of the nature of the "business";

   c. Arising out of the rental or holding for rental of any part of any premises by an "insured." This exclusion does not apply to the rental or holding for rental of an "insured location":

      (1) On an occasional basis if used only as a residence;

      (2) In part for use only as a residence, unless a single family unit is intended for use by the occupying family to lodge more than two roomers or boarders; or

      (3) In part, as an office, school, studio or private garage;

d. Arising out of the rendering of or failure to render professional services;

e. Arising out of a premises:

    (1) Owned by an "insured";

    (2) Rented to an "insured"; or

    (3) Rented to others by an "insured";

    that is not an "insured location";

f. Arising out of:

    (1) The ownership, maintenance, use, loading or unloading of motor vehicles or all other motorized land conveyances, including trailers, owned or operated by or rented or loaned to an "insured";

    (2) The entrustment by an "insured" of a motor vehicle or any other motorized land conveyance to any person; or

    (3) Vicarious liability, whether or not statutorily imposed, for the actions of a child or minor using a conveyance excluded in paragraph **(1)** or **(2)** above.

This exclusion does not apply to:

    (1) A trailer not towed by or carried on a motorized land conveyance;

    (2) A motorized land conveyance designed for recreational use off public roads, not subject to motor vehicle registration and:

      (a) Not owned by an "insured"; or

      (b) Owned by an "insured" and on an "insured location";

    (3) A motorized golf cart when used to play golf on a golf course;

    (4) A vehicle or conveyance not subject to motor vehicle registration which is:

      (a) Used to service an "insured's" residence;

      (b) Designed for assisting the handicapped; or

      (c) In dead storage on an "insured location";

g. Arising out of:

    (1) The ownership, maintenance, use, loading or unloading of an excluded watercraft described below;

    (2) The entrustment by an "insured" of an excluded watercraft described below to any person; or

    (3) Vicarious liability, whether or not statutorily imposed, for the actions of a child or minor using an excluded watercraft described below.

Excluded watercraft are those that are principally designed to be propelled by engine power or electric motor, or are sailing vessels, whether owned by or rented to an "insured." This exclusion does not apply to watercraft:

(1) That are not sailing vessels and are powered by:

    (a) Inboard or inboard-outdrive engine or motor power of 50 horsepower or less not owned by an "insured";

    (b) Inboard or inboard-outdrive engine or motor power of more than 50 horsepower not owned by or rented to an "insured";

    (c) One or more outboard engines or motors with 25 total horsepower or less;

    (d) One or more outboard engines or motors with more than 25 total horsepower if the outboard engine or motor is not owned by an "insured";

    (e) Outboard engines or motors of more than 25 total horsepower owned by an "insured" if:

      (i) You acquire them prior to the policy period; and

        (a) You declare them at policy inception; or

        (b) Your intention to insure is reported to us in writing within 45 days after you acquire the outboard engines or motors.

      (ii) You acquire them during the policy period.

    This coverage applies for the policy period.

(2) That are sailing vessels, with or without auxiliary power:

    (a) Less than 26 feet in overall length;

    (b) 26 feet or more in overall length, not owned by or rented to an "insured."

(3) That are stored;

h. Arising out of:

    (1) The ownership, maintenance, use, loading or unloading of an aircraft;

    (2) The entrustment by an "insured" of an aircraft to any person; or

    (3) Vicarious liability, whether or not statutorily imposed, for the actions of a child or minor using an aircraft.

An aircraft means any contrivance used or designed for flight, except model or hobby aircraft not used or designed to carry people or cargo;

i. Caused directly or indirectly by war, including the following and any consequence of any of the following:

  (1) Undeclared war, civil war, insurrection, rebellion or revolution;

  (2) Warlike act by a military force or military personnel; or

  (3) Destruction, seizure or use for a military purpose.

  Discharge of a nuclear weapon will be deemed a warlike act even if accidental;

j. Which arises out of the transmission of a communicable disease by an "insured";

k. Arising out of sexual molestation, corporal punishment or physical or mental abuse; or

l. Arising out of the use, sale, manufacture, delivery, transfer or possession by any person of a Controlled Substance(s) as defined by the Federal Food and Drug Law at 21 U.S.C.A. Sections 811 and 812. Controlled Substances include but are not limited to cocaine, LSD, marijuana and all narcotic drugs. However, this exclusion does not apply to the legitimate use of prescription drugs by a person following the orders of a licensed physician.

Exclusions **e.**, **f.**, **g.**, and **h.** do not apply to "bodily injury" to a "residence employee" arising out of and in the course of the "residence employee's" employment by an "insured".

2. **Coverage E – Personal Liability**, does not apply to:

a. Liability

  (1) For any loss assessment charged against you as a member of an association, corporation or community of property owners;

  (2) Under any contract or agreement. However, this exclusion does not apply to written contracts:

    (a) That directly relate to the ownership, maintenance or use of an "insured location"; or

    (b) Where the liability of others is assumed by the "insured" prior to an "occurrence";

    unless excluded in **(1)** above or elsewhere in this policy;

b. "Property damage" to property owned by the "insured";

c. "Property damage" to property rented to, occupied or used by or in the care of the "insured." This exclusion does not apply to "property damage" caused by fire, smoke or explosion;

d. "Bodily injury" to any person eligible to receive any benefits:

  (1) Voluntarily provided; or

  (2) Required to be provided;

  by the "insured" under any:

  (1) Workers' compensation law;

  (2) Non-occupational disability law; or

  (3) Occupational disease law;

e. "Bodily injury" or "property damage" for which an "insured" under this policy:

  (1) Is also an insured under a nuclear energy liability policy; or

  (2) Would be an insured under that policy but for the exhaustion of its limit of liability.

  A nuclear energy liability policy is one issued by:

  (1) American Nuclear Insurers;

  (2) Mutual Atomic Energy Liability Underwriters;

  (3) Nuclear Insurance Association of Canada;

  or any of their successors; or

f. "Bodily injury" to you or an "insured" within the meaning of part **a.** or **b.** of "insured" as defined.

3. **Coverage F – Medical Payments to Others,** does not apply to "bodily injury":

a. To a "residence employee" if the "bodily injury":

  (1) Occurs off the "insured location"; and

  (2) Does not arise out of or in the course of the "residence employee's" employment by an "insured";

b. To any person eligible to receive benefits:

  (1) Voluntarily provided; or

  (2) Required to be provided;

  under any:

  (1) Workers' compensation law;

  (2) Non-occupational disability law; or

  (3) Occupational disease law;

 HO 00 06 04 91

c. From any:

   (1) Nuclear reaction;

   (2) Nuclear radiation; or

   (3) Radioactive contamination;

   all whether controlled or uncontrolled or however caused; or

(4) Any consequence of any of these; or

d. To any person, other than a "residence employee" of an "insured," regularly residing on any part of the "insured location."

SECTION II – ADDITIONAL COVERAGES

We cover the following in addition to the limits of liability:

1. Claim Expenses. We pay:

a. Expenses we incur and costs taxed against an "insured" in any suit we defend;

b. Premiums on bonds required in a suit we defend, but not for bond amounts more than the limit of liability for Coverage E. We need not apply for or furnish any bond;

c. Reasonable expenses incurred by an "insured" at our request, including actual loss of earnings (but not loss of other income) up to $50 per day, for assisting us in the investigation or defense of a claim or suit; and

d. Interest on the entire judgment which accrues after entry of the judgment and before we pay or tender, or deposit in court that part of the judgment which does not exceed the limit of liability that applies.

2. First Aid Expenses. We will pay expenses for first aid to others incurred by an "insured" for "bodily injury" covered under this policy. We will not pay for first aid to you or any other "insured."

3. Damage to Property of Others. We will pay at replacement cost, up to $500 per "occurrence" for "property damage" to property of others caused by an "insured."

We will not pay for "property damage":

a. To the extent of any amount recoverable under Section I of this policy;

b. Caused intentionally by an "insured" who is 13 years of age or older;

c. To property owned by an "insured";

d. To property owned by or rented to a tenant of an "insured" or a resident in your household; or

e. Arising out of:

   (1) A "business" engaged in by an "insured";

   (2) Any act or omission in connection with a premises owned, rented or controlled by an "insured," other than the "insured location"; or

   (3) The ownership, maintenance, or use of aircraft, watercraft or motor vehicles or all other motorized land conveyances.

   This exclusion does not apply to a motorized land conveyance designed for recreational use off public roads, not subject to motor vehicle registration and not owned by an "insured."

4. Loss Assessment. We will pay up to $1000 for your share of loss assessment charged during the policy period against you by a corporation or association of property owners, when the assessment is made as a result of:

a. "Bodily injury" or "property damage" not excluded under Section II of this policy; or

b. Liability for an act of a director, officer or trustee in the capacity as a director, officer or trustee, provided:

   (1) The director, officer or trustee is elected by the members of a corporation or association of property owners; and

   (2) The director, officer or trustee serves without deriving any income from the exercise of duties which are solely on behalf of a corporation or association of property owners.

This coverage applies only to loss assessments charged against you as owner or tenant of the "residence premises."

We do not cover loss assessments charged against you or a corporation or association of property owners by any governmental body.

Regardless of the number of assessments, the limit of $1000 is the most we will pay for loss arising out of:

a. One accident, including continuous or repeated exposure to substantially the same general harmful condition; or

b. A covered act of a director, officer or trustee. An act involving more than one director, officer or trustee is considered to be a single act.

The following do not apply to this coverage:

1. Section II – Coverage E – Personal Liability Exclusion **2.a.(1)**;

2. Condition **1.** Policy Period, under SECTIONS I AND II CONDITIONS.

SECTION II – CONDITIONS

1. **Limit of Liability.** Our total liability under Coverage E for all damages resulting from any one "occurrence" will not be more than the limit of liability for Coverage E as shown in the Declarations. This limit is the same regardless of the number of "insureds," claims made or persons injured. All "bodily injury" and "property damage" resulting from any one accident or from continuous or repeated exposure to substantially the same general harmful conditions shall be considered to be the result of one "occurrence."

   Our total liability under Coverage F for all medical expense payable for "bodily injury" to one person as the result of one accident will not be more than the limit of liability for Coverage F as shown in the Declarations.

2. **Severability of Insurance.** This insurance applies separately to each "insured." This condition will not increase our limit of liability for any one "occurrence."

3. **Duties After Loss.** In case of an accident or "occurrence," the "insured" will perform the following duties that apply. You will help us by seeing that these duties are performed:

   a. Give written notice to us or our agent as soon as is practical, which sets forth:

      (1) The identity of the policy and "insured";

      (2) Reasonably available information on the time, place and circumstances of the accident or "occurrence"; and

      (3) Names and addresses of any claimants and witnesses;

   b. Promptly forward to us every notice, demand, summons or other process relating to the accident or "occurrence";

   c. At our request, help us:

      (1) To make settlement;

      (2) To enforce any right of contribution or indemnity against any person or organization who may be liable to an "insured";

      (3) With the conduct of suits and attend hearings and trials; and

      (4) To secure and give evidence and obtain the attendance of witnesses;

   d. Under the coverage – Damage to Property of Others – submit to us within 60 days after the loss, a sworn statement of loss and show the damaged property, if in the "insured's" control;

   e. The "insured" will not, except at the "insured's" own cost, voluntarily make payment, assume obligation or incur expense other than for first aid to others at the time of the "bodily injury."

4. **Duties of an Injured Person – Coverage F – Medical Payments to Others.**

   The injured person or someone acting for the injured person will:

   a. Give us written proof of claim, under oath if required, as soon as is practical; and

   b. Authorize us to obtain copies of medical reports and records.

   The injured person will submit to a physical exam by a doctor of our choice when and as often as we reasonably require.

5. **Payment of Claim – Coverage F – Medical Payments to Others.** Payment under this coverage is not an admission of liability by an "insured" or us.

6. **Suit Against Us.** No action can be brought against us unless there has been compliance with the policy provisions.

   No one will have the right to join us as a party to any action against an "insured." Also, no action with respect to Coverage E can be brought against us until the obligation of the "insured" has been determined by final judgment or agreement signed by us.

7. **Bankruptcy of an Insured.** Bankruptcy or insolvency of an "insured" will not relieve us of our obligations under this policy.

8. **Other Insurance – Coverage E – Personal Liability.** This insurance is excess over other valid and collectible insurance except insurance written specifically to cover as excess over the limits of liability that apply in this policy.

 HO 00 06 04 91

SECTIONS I AND II – CONDITIONS

1. **Policy Period.** This policy applies only to loss in Section I or "bodily injury" or "property damage" in Section II, which occurs during the policy period.

2. **Concealment or Fraud.** The entire policy will be void if, whether before or after a loss, an "insured" has:

   a. Intentionally concealed or misrepresented any material fact or circumstance;

   b. Engaged in fraudulent conduct; or

   c. Made false statements;

   relating to this insurance.

3. **Liberalization Clause.** If we make a change which broadens coverage under this edition of our policy without additional premium charge, that change will automatically apply to your insurance as of the date we implement the change in your state, provided that this implementation date falls within 60 days prior to or during the policy period stated in the Declarations.

   This Liberalization Clause does not apply to changes implemented through introduction of a subsequent edition of our policy.

4. **Waiver or Change of Policy Provisions.**

   A waiver or change of a provision of this policy must be in writing by us to be valid. Our request for an appraisal or examination will not waive any of our rights.

5. **Cancellation.**

   a. You may cancel this policy at any time by returning it to us or by letting us know in writing of the date cancellation is to take effect.

   b. We may cancel this policy only for the reasons stated below by letting you know in writing of the date cancellation takes effect. This cancellation notice may be delivered to you, or mailed to you at your mailing address shown in the Declarations.

      Proof of mailing will be sufficient proof of notice.

      (1) When you have not paid the premium, we may cancel at any time by letting you know at least 10 days before the date cancellation takes effect.

      (2) When this policy has been in effect for less than 60 days and is not a renewal with us, we may cancel for any reason by letting you know at least 10 days before the date cancellation takes effect.

      (3) When this policy has been in effect for 60 days or more, or at any time if it is a renewal with us, we may cancel:

         (a) If there has been a material misrepresentation of fact which if known to us would have caused us not to issue the policy; or

         (b) If the risk has changed substantially since the policy was issued.

         This can be done by letting you know at least 30 days before the date cancellation takes effect.

      (4) When this policy is written for a period of more than one year, we may cancel for any reason at anniversary by letting you know at least 30 days before the date cancellation takes effect.

   c. When this policy is cancelled, the premium for the period from the date of cancellation to the expiration date will be refunded pro rata.

   d. If the return premium is not refunded with the notice of cancellation or when this policy is returned to us, we will refund it within a reasonable time after the date cancellation takes effect.

6. **Nonrenewal.** We may elect not to renew this policy. We may do so by delivering to you, or mailing to you at your mailing address shown in the Declarations, written notice at least 30 days before the expiration date of this policy. Proof of mailing will be sufficient proof of notice.

7. **Assignment.** Assignment of this policy will not be valid unless we give our written consent.

8. **Subrogation.** An "insured" may waive in writing before a loss all rights of recovery against any person. If not waived, we may require an assignment of rights of recovery for a loss to the extent that payment is made by us.

   If an assignment is sought, an "insured" must sign and deliver all related papers and cooperate with us.

   Subrogation does not apply under Section II to Medical Payments to Others or Damage to Property of Others.

9. **Death.** If any person named in the Declarations or the spouse, if a resident of the same household, dies:

   a. We insure the legal representative of the deceased but only with respect to the premises and property of the deceased covered under the policy at the time of death;

b. "Insured" includes:

   (1) Any member of your household who is an "insured" at the time of your death, but only while a resident of the "residence premises"; and

   (2) With respect to your property, the person having proper temporary custody of the property until appointment and qualification of a legal representative.

 HO 00 06 04 91

Index

A

S

settlements
  as contracts 1

U

uncertainty
  in contracting 9, 18–19, 39–40